THE
STUDENT
JOURNALIST
GUIDE
SERIES

REVIEWING THE PERFORMING ARTS

by
SAMUEL L. SINGER

PUBLISHED BY
RICHARDS ROSEN
PRESS, INC.
NEW YORK

To my wife,
ELIZABETH,

the best critic
in the Singer family

Standard Book Number: 8239-0287-0
Library of Congress Catalog Card Number: 73-80359
Dewey Decimal Classification: 371.897

Published in 1974 by Richards Rosen Press, Inc.
29 East 21st Street, New York City, N.Y. 10010

Copyright 1974 by Samuel L. Singer

All rights reserved. No part of this book may be reproduced in any form without written permission from the publisher, except by a reviewer.

First Edition

Manufactured in the United States of America

The Student Journalist
and
REVIEWING THE
PERFORMING ARTS

THE STUDENT JOURNALIST AND

ABOUT THE AUTHOR

Samuel L. Singer has reviewed thousands of concerts, hundreds of operas, plays, movies, dance events, television programs, and everything else from ice shows to the Lipizzaner horses, since he joined the staff of *The Philadelphia Inquirer* in 1934. Dean of Philadelphia reviewers, he has been music editor of the newspaper for more than twenty years.

Adjunct professor of communications in the School of Communications and Theater of Temple University, his alma mater, Singer has taught reviewing to journalism students for almost thirty years. He has had graduate classes in music criticism in the College of Music at Temple University. He says he makes "expert reviewers in twenty-five easy lessons." Many of his "alumni" now review cultural events on newspapers, large and small, across the United States.

Although he had to be persuaded by his former journalism professor to try his hand at teaching, Singer has loved it from the first. He says teaching college students keeps him young.

A lifelong resident of his native Philadelphia, except for "two and three-quarters years and seven hours" in the Navy in World War II, Singer is also a church organist and choir director. He is married and has three children, all of whom have some musical and journalistic proclivities.

ACKNOWLEDGMENTS

I am grateful for helpful criticism of the manuscript, or for practical suggestions on specific chapters, to my good friends Robert S. Bookhammer, M.D. and Nathaniel Lieberman; my former *Philadelphia Inquirer* colleague, Henry T. Murdock, retired drama and motion picture critic, and to Professor Kenneth Starck, of the Southern Illinois University department of journalism.

Thanks, too, to my former Temple University colleague, Professor Paul S. Swensson, for copyreading an entire "script"; to Misses Marianne Galvin and Linda LuBow, of the journalism secretarial staff, and my daughter, Ruth B. Singer, for typing and duplicating the manuscript for prepublication use in my classes.

S. L. S.

CONTENTS

	Acknowledgments	12
	Foreword	15
I.	A Good Critic	17
II.	An Arts Event Is News	19
III.	Some Technical Suggestions	21
IV.	Components of Criticism: The Critic Himself	27
V.	Components of Criticism: Direct Data—Material, Form, and Workmanship	33
VI.	Components of Criticism: Indirect Data	40
VII.	General Structure of a Play Review	45
VIII.	Avant-garde Theater	53
IX.	Reviewing Movies	55
X.	Musical Comedies	60
XI.	New Play Versus Old Play: How the Reviews Differ; Operettas	63
XII.	Television Reviewing	68
XIII.	Review the Work at Hand	76
XIV.	Music Reviewing: T'NT and the Solo Artist	78
XV.	Instrumental and Vocal Ensembles—and Conductors	87
XVI.	Grand Opera	95
XVII.	Folk and Rock Music	103
XVIII.	Popular and Classical Music: Shall the Twain Ever Meet?—Music by Chance	107
XIX.	Ballet and the Modern Dance	109

Contents

XX.	Book Reviewing	119
XXI.	Record Reviewing	126
XXII.	Art Criticism	131
XXIII.	Covering the Hometown Performer	138
XXIV.	Finale: Opportunities and Pitfalls	142

Appendices

A.	A Basic Glossary of Adjectives and Adverbs	145
B.	Stage and Film Terms	148
C.	A Basic Musical Glossary	150
D.	A Basic Ballet Glossary	159
E.	Television and Radio Terms	161
F.	Arts Periodicals Published in the United States	163
G.	Examples of Play Reviews	167
H.	Biographical Data	179

FOREWORD

The Approach to This Book from a Newspaperman's Point of View

Writing for a newspaper of daily or less frequent publication is the most common form of journalism. Therefore, this book will discuss the reviewing of plays, movies, television, musical events, the dance, books, and art from the point of view of a reviewer for a metropolitan daily.

Sometimes reviews for a small town or college newspaper may differ in detail, in points emphasized (especially when there is a local angle), and these differences will be treated separately. But the principles are much the same for any arts event reviewed. The things one looks for remain the same; the difference is in how strictly the standards are applied.

An oral review, for television or radio, may differ from a written one. Here, too, it is hoped this book will serve as a guidepost, with details adapted to the broadcasting medium.

This book is being written with college students in mind. It also may be of use to general reporters who aspire to add a specialty to their equipment, and it may even be read profitably by high school students.

Since it is an elementary textbook, there is bound to be some repetition. The conversational style is the outgrowth of a quarter of a century of teaching—and learning from—journalism students at Temple University in Philadelphia.

Samuel L. Singer

Chapter I

A GOOD CRITIC

"How'd you like the movie?"
"It was swell!"
"I thought it was lousy."
(Today: "Boss" or "cool"; "drag" or "hairy.")
Such capsule and colloquial criticisms of any lively arts event—movie, play, TV show, or concert—are common. But only orally. A speaker can get away with a criticism of a show that may be as concise as the above.

But a writer for a newspaper or any other periodical, or a broadcaster, not only is generally forbidden by good taste to use such words as "swell" or "lousy." He has to use more than one word. He may have to use as many as 250 or 300 or 400 or more. His words must be reasoned and organized. Worse yet, if he expresses any opinion—and he is expected to—his words must buttress his opinions. Nothing is more disconcerting to the reader than when a reviewer contradicts himself.

Whereas a general reporter, covering a fire or a speech, has facts in hand and can organize his story from the "Five W's," a critic must pick words out of the air, so to speak. His opinions are usually the main points of his story. While general reporters deal with nouns and verbs, the most interesting words in a review are the adjectives and adverbs.

What to look for, how to find the right words, how to organize them: that is the purpose of this book.

It is a practical book, not a theoretical one. It treats little of the theory of criticism, or its place in the social order. It avoids the aesthetics of criticism, whatever they are.

The critic, said Oscar Thompson, holds a mirror to the performance, but it is an intensifying mirror, showing the highlights and omitting immaterial details. The reviewer should summarize the performance so well that he not only satisfies the man who wasn't there, but adds something to the overall impression, perhaps by some enlivening details, of the man who was.

Right now might be a good time to distinguish between the words "critic" and "reviewer." In this book, the words are used interchangeably, but we really are talking about reviewers.

As critic Stephen Koch pointed out in the *Saturday Review*,* "The word critic is widely misused. A true critic is not necessarily a reviewer; a reviewer is not necessarily a critic—in fact, rarely is. Each has his rightful place, but they are really quite different breeds of cat.

"The reviewer is fundamentally a newsman, and the review is basically a piece of news, what the French would call an intellectual *fait divers*. He is temperamentally very different from the critic, who is really a kind of garden-variety philosopher. The reviewer's strong points are speed, topicality, wit, and fact. The critic publishes several months after the reviewer has forgotten what the movie was even about; his virtues are long meditation, a firm historical sense, profound insight, truth—even truth with a capital T.

"The two write in different ways, in different places, for different audiences. The critic's audience finds the reviewer flashy and cheap, the past master of the snap judgment. The reviewer's audience finds the critic dull and overly elaborate. They operate on different levels, they think in different ways, and they rarely get along very well. There is, of course, a shadow line between the two; the same person can sometimes do both jobs, sometimes even fuse the two activities—though even Shaw found that one tough. Generally, confusing the two creates only confusion."

A critic's arguments, says Koch, may even change a reader's mind. A review will rarely have that effect, says the author of this textbook—but it will help make up the mind of the reader who waits to see the newspaper review before he knows what he thinks of the movie, play, or concert he attended the night before.

What is a good critic?

I have always given a cynical answer: "A good critic is one who agrees with you." This is in jocular reference to your daily reader—if he agrees with what you said about the movie he saw, you're a good critic; if not, you're a bum.

A good critic, however, is read. He should write well enough to interest the casual reader, and, hopefully, convincingly enough to impress the man who was there, too.

---

* *Saturday Review*, Dec. 26, 1970.

Chapter II

AN ARTS EVENT IS NEWS

A critic is first of all a reporter. The events he covers are news of a specialized nature; therefore, the articles seldom are written so that they can be cut from the end when necessary, like many news dispatches.

A straight news story usually has the most important facts in the lead, the succeeding paragraphs tapering off in importance. A review also has a certain general construction. As with any good news story, the lead should be as interesting as possible. It usually incorporates four of the five W's—what, where, when, who, why—and how!

The "where" and "when" are usually perfunctory—the theater or concert hall, and "last night." The "who," of course, is variable. If it is a solo artist such as Van Cliburn or Zino Francescatti, it may be a one-word identification—"pianist" or "violinist," or a few words may be added to refresh the reader's memory or to introduce the artist to a reader who chances on the review without having heard of this world-famous fellow. If the artist is making his local debut, concise identification is mandatory. But remember that your article is a review, not a biography.

The same remarks apply to a play, movie, or television review. In the case of Shakespeare or Shaw (Bernard, not Irwin), the name alone would usually be sufficient identification. The review of a first play, however, should include a few words about the playwright. And, of course, it is news when a first play is a hit.

Identification of actors, players, producers—in movies, plays, or television—all vary according to the familiarity to the reader of your article, with an elaboration of the "what." In a recital or opera, you would be telling what was performed and how it was done. For a play or movie, the same.

The "why" does not always figure—overtly, that is—in a review. Ordinarily, the performance is given because it's given. It may be part of a series, and that is worth mentioning. It may be in commemoration of some event—the 400th birthday anniversary of Shakespeare—or it may be a special performance for a convention. This would be a "why" for you.

On the other hand, it may be a new play that is so bad you wonder in print why on earth anyone would produce such drivel. There may be other occasions when the "why" pops up, almost always closely tied in with the "what" and "how."

The review should tell all the "news" of the event—in other words, anything worthy of mention. Depending on the individual newspaper and the availability of space, the reviewer may write as much (or as little) as he chooses, or he may be restricted to a certain space. In the latter case, his words must be chosen sparingly, and he may even have to omit certain details.

Chapter III

SOME TECHNICAL SUGGESTIONS

Neither a general reporter nor a reviewer is a stenographer. An article by neither should include every detail of every event. The report of a speech does not contain every word the speaker said. You may take more notes on the performance than you have need or room for; you choose the more important items and omit the rest.

Rarely will you report a concert or play "inning by inning," in the order of performance. Writing nothing except the synopsis of a play or movie would bore the reader (if he even bothers to read that far), and it is not necessary to speak of the compositions in a concert in the order they were performed, except as a matter of convenience or logic.

When given a specific amount of space for his review, the experienced reporter tries to write to fit the space. For instance, three or three and a half or four typewritten lines may make one inch of type in the average newspaper column. Ten inches for a review would mean about thirty-five typewritten lines or 350 words. Some writers set their typewriters for the number of units in their paper's type line. Some editors insist on it.

Sometimes the reporter will write exactly enough. This may happen with gratifying frequency. At other times his copy will run a little short. Then it may be "leaded out" (a mechanical process), or if it is too short, a "filler" (short article) will be used to fit the space. (If you are lucky, there will be a "short" waiting on the type bank about some phase of the amusement field; a related story is always acceptable. But just as often, the compositor, racing against deadline, will grab the first short handy—"300 Die in Flood in India" or "Upstate Man Held in Theft." It doesn't look right on the amusement page, but the space must be filled.)

What happens if you write too much? This can be coped with in two ways.

As mentioned before, a review is not generally written to be chopped at the end, paragraph by paragraph. If you doubt whether your story will stay in the allotted space, and you can go to the composing room, you can wait until the story is set in type and the page is ready to be made up. Then you can make your own trims as necessary. Or you can leave a carbon copy of your review with the makeup editor, with suggested cuts. Left to his own devices—or vices—the makeup man might cut off the last paragraph of your review, thereby eliminating mention of the accompanist or the supporting cast or some of the stage or screen credits. Or, horror of horrors, your witty tagline.

A more pragmatic method, when you are uncertain about "hitting it right" in an allotted space, is to write a throwaway paragraph, a sentence or two, that will be quite acceptable in the story, but that never will be missed if trimmed. Such a paragraph could name additional minor members of a cast, or mention the next event in the concert or opera series, or even be some additional although nonvital comment. General news reporters often write an optional tail-end paragraph; there is no reason why reviewers cannot, when necessary.

About taking notes: there are two schools of thought. Some reviewers take no notes at all during a performance, feeling that any point important enough to mention will come to mind when the critic sits down at the typewriter.

This may work for some reviewers. But from my forty years' experience in covering performances in all the lively arts, my suggestion is: Take notes. They need not be lengthy; usually a word or two will call to mind a sentence or a paragraph at the typewriter. But the words you write down are important. They usually will be more apposite, more pungent, than if you depend on memory for details. Of course, you can transmit the general effect of any performance, without notes, to your readers. But the notes you take will add spice to your review. Moreover, they will make your job easier. You will not be worried, consciously or subconsciously, about remembering details; your notes will jog your memory where it needs to be jogged —at the typewriter.

Also, if you plan to quote a line or two from the play or movie you're reviewing, the written word is more accurate than memory.

How does one take notes in a dark theater or concert hall?

There usually will be light enough, from the stage or otherwise, for you to see to write those pertinent words on your program. You may use a penlight or pocket flashlight. Shield such a light from distracting your neighbor.

Some reviewers carry a stenographer's notebook or a pad of copy paper. This allows enough expanse so that you can write in the dark without looking at the paper as you write. But be sure not to write over what you have already written—it is disconcertingly difficult to decipher it later!

(Parenthetically, some interviewers pride themselves on not taking notes for fear their subject will not speak as freely. This is unlikely. If an actor or political figure is being interviewed, he knows he is talking for publication. The reporter may rush to the office and write out what he remembers, but it would be more accurate—and more reassuring to the interviewee—for the reporter to get quotes verbatim. Here, too, a reporter's general impression of what was said is no substitute for pithy and pictorial expressions used by the subject.)

It may seem unnecessary to mention here other recommended practices, such as typing your reviews double-spaced, allowing sufficient margin on all sides for copy editing, and not continuing a paragraph from one page to the next. (This is because different Linotypists may set each page.) It is considered good form for a reviewer to spell names and titles correctly.

Copyread your own review before surrendering it to the editor or the copydesk. A reviewer is a specialist; as such his copy is less liable to tampering—if he is dependable in spelling and facts. If a fellow reviewer is around when you have finished your article, and there is sufficient time before deadline, ask him to look over your copy (and you may read his). Too often you won't spot your own error, typographical or otherwise, until it jumps at you from tomorrow's paper. A confrere may save you such embarrassment. (You are less liable to spot your own typo because your eyes read what you want them to read. This is psychological.)

Sometimes a critic attends a play or concert in a suburb or city too distant for him to go back to the office to write his review. Unlike the sportswriter, he does not have a telegraph wire handy. He is usually forced to telephone his review. Here, if time permits, it would be well to ask the unfortunate rewrite man, who has taken your dictated review, to read it back to you on the telephone. The boners, between what you said and what the man at the other end thinks you said, can fill a scrapbook. (One recent example: "The tenor sang with feeling, and did not tear the drama to shreds" came out ". . . with feeling, but missed the dramatic thread.")

It is a good idea to submit an extra copy of the program with your review. This way, the copyreader can check on spelling of names and titles. Be sure, however, that you first correct any typographical errors or changes of cast or program. Another good habit is to underline lightly and mark "OK," in your review, any names with an unusual spelling (Rozhdestvensky or Donavon, for instance).

The practice will vary with the writer, the periodical, and the experience of the individual, but ordinarily a pronoun referring to the critic should not intrude in the review. That is, eschew the use of the first person, singular or plural.

Admittedly, there is sharp difference of opinion on this. The author's view is this: You are speaking for your newspaper, and avoiding the first-person pronoun makes your review appear more factual rather than one person's statement of opinion. It goes without saying that your review, although thus stated as fact, is indeed one man's opinion. But it carries more weight when expressed in impersonal terms.

To use "I" or "we" in a review calls attention to yourself and proclaims that this is one man's opinion that the newspaper is printing. Of course it is! But you need not hit the reader over the head to emphasize this fact.

A special point for new reviewers: Wait to use the first person until you have been writing reviews awhile and have established something of a reputation with your readers. The first person—if you insist on using it—may mean something then.

In similar vein, sometimes you may not be sure of your opinion and you want to hedge a bit. You will be tempted to use some such phrase as "in this reviewer's opinion." This serves only to weaken the review. Leave it out and let your review speak for itself.

Words are the reviewer's stock in trade. The bigger his vocabulary, the better equipped he is. He should be able to express himself precisely, conveying any fine distinction that he wants to convey.

On the other hand, there are two faults the reviewer should avoid in his writing. He should not be a virtuoso writer, using flamboyant phrases for their own sake, or a cruel witticism that is just too good to pass up even if it does an injustice to writer or performer. Nor should he send readers to the dictionary.

He should not use esoteric words or technical terms that are understood by only a minority of his readers. He should bear in mind the publication for which he is writing. Words that would fit easily into a musical or theatrical publication should be translated or stated more generally in a daily newspaper.

The preceding chapter stated that "a critic is first of all a reporter." This means that he is responsible for reporting anything that goes on at the event he is covering. The extracurricular occurrence may or may not have a bearing on the performance. It may or may not be included in the review, and/or it may become a "sidebar" story. This is left to the judgment of the reviewer and his city editor.

For instance, if an actor falls ill during the performance, this certainly is mentioned. If someone else stands in for him, holding the script in hand, this will affect the performance. Meanwhile, another reporter will check on the actor's condition at the hospital.

The incident may be humorous and may not affect the performance at all, yet it must be mentioned and may even be worth a picture (in that case, phone quickly for a photographer). Once, during a two-piano recital at the Philadelphia Academy of Music by the great team of Pierre Luboshutz and Genia Nemenoff, a dog walked slowly onto the stage and lay down on Mme. Nemenoff's pedaling foot. The audience tittered. The pianists never missed a beat.

During intermission, it developed that the pianists, fearing "Vodka" would be lonesome in the hotel room, brought the dog to their dressing room. But they neglected to close the door, and when "Vodka" heard the music, naturally he wanted to be with his mistress. This made a bright lead for the review and provided a good picture, too.

A sidebar story, with mere mention in the review, developed when several pieces of plaster fell into the orchestra-level audience during an opera performance at the Academy of Music. No one was hurt, and the audience in the vicinity scattered. This, one suspects, led to the multimillion-dollar restoration and modernization of the century-old concert hall.

The weather or the crowd may be important facets of your story—especially at a rock festival!

Always, the reviewer must weigh all points and decide which ones to use, theatrical, musical, or otherwise, and in what proportion.

Proportion—that's a good thing to keep in mind. And it brings us to one final point in our technical discussion.

The points at the beginning and ending of a review often carry more weight than if placed deeper in the story. Therefore, do not start or end with an observation that is an exception to your general premise.

Should you start appraising a show or musical event by listing the shortcomings, and then go on to praise the show as a whole, your reader may get the wrong idea of your opinion—especially if he doesn't read the entire review. Most newspaper readers are scanners—and this applies to readers of reviews as well as readers of the news pages.

Near the end of your review, when you are discussing details, do not close with an exception to your main premise. You may be talking about a star's performance or supporting actors' performances. "Miss Smith's portrayal of the schoolteacher was completely convincing. She conveyed every nuance of the character. But her wig was on crooked."

The matter of the wig, obviously, was less important than Miss Smith's acting. Better to surround mention of the wig with more positive phrases: ". . . completely convincing. Despite the fact that her wig was on crooked, she conveyed every nuance of the character."

Or in a recital review: "The violinist played his final group of pieces with technical flair that provided a brilliant ending to the recital. But his intonation was faulty in the last Paganini Caprice." To end on this tone is disproportionate. Better: "The final group of pieces were played with a technical flair that, despite faulty intonation in the last Paganini Caprice, provided a brilliant ending to the recital."

The same advice applies when you express general disapproval but mention one or two good points. Do not end with the exception.

Chapter IV

COMPONENTS OF CRITICISM: THE CRITIC HIMSELF

M. D. Calvocoressi, distinguished Greek-French author and critic, was among the first to analyze the components of musical criticism (*The Principles and Methods of Musical Criticism,* Oxford University Press, 1923). He noted three major factors in appraising a work of music, which we may apply to appraising any work of art: direct data, everything present in the music (or other creative work) itself; indirect data, knowledge surrounding the work itself—history, the author's statements (or disclaimers) of intention, comparison with similar works by the same or other authors; and what has been termed "predispositions"—the critic himself.

In writing about anything whatsoever, the reporter acts as a funnel. In reporting a speech, he chooses what to quote and in what order. The speaker himself may regard a quotation other than that used in the "lead" as his most important statement. But the reporter's judgment, embodied in his sense of news values, prevails. All that the readers of the newspaper know about that speech is what the reporter has chosen—presumably using his best judgment—to give them. Of course, the reader may see another newspaper, or hear a radio report of the speech, or get a snatch of it on television. Thereby John Q. Public may round out his picture of the event reported. He may get more than one viewpoint. The various reports may agree in general, but they may differ sharply in detail or perspective.

The reviewer similarly acts as a funnel for his readers (or listeners). He will give his audience as true a critique as is humanly possible. Note that he is human (musicians, producers, and playwrights to the contrary). First of all, there is the critic's background—his taste, inborn and/or acquired (of this, more later); his likes and dislikes, prejudices for and against, his emotional stability—even his disposition that evening. A deep personal problem, an illness, perhaps a quarrel with his wife—may put him in no mood for a comedy. Should he be reviewing a comedy that night, the play might suffer at his hands; the same plot that he would find, on another occasion, quite amusing, despite its light content, he may pan without giving it a second thought.

But this time he should give it a second thought. He should be aware of his out-of-sorts feeling that night. The experienced critic will probably do this subconsciously, as a matter of habit. He will be asking himself, perhaps not in so many words, "If I felt better, would I be praising this play instead of panning it?" In the unlikely event that the answer is in the affirmative, the critic would reappraise his reactions to the play before writing his review.

At one time or another, you have heard someone say (or you may have said it yourself), "I don't know much about art (or music), but I know what I like." Can you imagine the state of the arts if critics in their writing followed this reasoning? A Philadelphia music critic goes a step further—"The public likes what it knows."

Certainly, the music-listening public is more likely to attend a Beethoven program than one of twenty-first century composers, or *La Bohème* instead of *Wozzeck*. It knows—and respects—Beethoven's music, whereas the work of avant-garde composers remains a fearsome mystery, which, however, may slowly catch on. It is possible that Alban Berg's *Wozzeck* may achieve recognition from the public for the masterpiece it is in another twenty or fifty or a hundred years. It is even possible that Puccini's music may be out of style in another century, just as the operas of Meyerbeer and Massenet, rulers of French opera a century ago, are out of fashion now.

All the critic's taste, background, and judgment go through another funnel, or filter: the writer's ability to express himself. It was noted in Chapter II that words are a reviewer's tools. He can add to his vocabulary by judicious reading. He can and should supplement his background of experience by achieving great knowledge about his chosen field—in theater, cinema, television, music, ballet, literature, art. Of course, all these fields have some relationship to one another. All that a critic needs to know is everything about every art, history, sociology, economics, philosophy, languages, and religion! But since all these attributes are obviously impossible to acquire within the

Components of Criticism: The Critic Himself 29

normal twenty-five-hour day and eight-day week of a conscientious critic, he does the best he can.

One method by which the critic improves himself comes with the job itself. He builds a background as he works. The greater his background, the firmer his base of standards. By seeing many plays or movies, by listening to many concerts, by reading many books, he strengthens his standards of judgment. He knows not only what has gone before, so that he is a better judge of originality and treatment (see next chapter), but he knows what standards can be achieved in writing and performance.

You do not remember the first time you saw a Western on television. You probably liked it. You were thrilled by the chases on horseback, the cloppity-clop, the gunplay. If the villain was injured, or killed, you may have thought it really happened. Most important of all, you did not know whether the goodies or the baddies would win.

After a few or many more television Westerns, and perhaps some in a movie theater, you came to realize that the villains didn't get shot for real ("it's just make-believe"), and that the goodies always beat the baddies, so you didn't have to worry about that any more. Then came the time when you may have tired of the conventional Western fare, and turned to "adult" and/or comedy Westerns, until they, too, began to pall.

Meanwhile, some Western programs maintained their popularity on television, while most others fell by the wayside after a season or two. Some had better writers, or a situation that provided more attention-holding variations on the basic plot.

Through the years you—along with millions of children and adults —thus became TV critics. True, you never thought of yourself as a TV critic. But you were and are. You and millions of others became critics with your first—well, let's say your second—TV Western, movie, play, concert, or art exhibit. The difference is that, of the millions who watch television or go to plays and concerts or who read books, only a comparatively few analyze their reactions. Still fewer write them down, in reasoned array, as critics for newspapers or other periodicals, as was suggested in Chapter I.

Turn to another analogy before tackling the elements that provide the direct data—the arts event that you are writing about. Consider a bowl of vegetable soup. A man who has had nothing to eat for a week would gulp the soup, whether hot or cold, and relish it. Someone who had never eaten vegetable soup might like it, or dislike it, immediately. Others of varying experience would like or dislike the soup in the degree molded by their tastes and habits.

How about a master chef? He would savor the soup as to temperature, seasoning, consistency, and ingredients. He would note the amounts of liquid, meat, and various vegetables, and whether they were cooked properly. Are the ingredients in the proper proportions? Are there too many potatoes, not enough meat, too much thin liquid? All in all, how good is this soup—and why?

Note that the chef, as a critic of soup, asks himself not only how good is the soup, but the reasons therefor.

When topical dramas, on stage or screen, or TV documentaries are concerned, the critic's predispositions are an important factor. Just how important depends on the critic's ability to detach himself emotionally from what he is reviewing long enough to assess his emotions as well as the play.

For example, a TV documentary on the civil-rights struggle may reap different critical reviews in the North and in the South. A northern writer with strong feelings in favor of aiding the black man may praise a documentary that a southern critic, perhaps sympathetic with white resistance to the black political upsurge there, may pan. Both writers may honestly be trying to assay the documentary purely on the plausibility of the arguments (if any): How well is each side presented, how convincingly, with what degree of fairness? Their own depth of feeling on this touchy subject may, however, warp their judgment of the presentation. The caution here is to judge the quality of the documentary, not the validity of the arguments presented. You are not, in your review, judging the merits of the civil-rights question —you are criticizing a TV documentary.

The same caution applies to nearly any controversial subject debated on television. Views on abortion or government aid to nonpublic schools are often colored by one's religious background. The reviewer should make sure that his own background and prejudices do not blind him to the merits or demerits of the program he is appraising.

One cannot divorce one's family or economic background, but the reviewer can be aware of his own predilections in considering a program dealing with our involvement in Southeast Asia, a state income tax, no-fault automobile insurance, or lowering of college standards to admit more members of minority groups. The list of controversial subjects is endless.

Earlier in this chapter, we mentioned the man who "knows what he likes." The caution here is not to dilute a critic's taste but to broaden it. Or, to put it another way, to judge a performance on its own terms.

For instance, you may like vanilla ice cream, but not strawberry. This is your privilege. But suppose you are, by mistake or otherwise, served some strawberry ice cream. You don't like strawberry ice cream; does this mean all strawberry ice cream is bad? No, and if you were appraising it, you would judge not only whether this is good ice cream, but how good a strawberry ice cream is it?

You are an "old-fashioned longhair"—you like classical music, but not folk music. Does this mean all folk singers are bad? They are not to your taste. But suppose you are sent to review a folk concert. You would judge the singers on how good they are as folk singers—not whether they compare to Birgit Nilsson or Cesare Siepi.

Your own preference is for organ or piano recitals, baritones or mezzo-sopranos. A little bit of a harpsichord, a guitar, a tenor, or a coloratura soprano—for you—goes a long way. You are sent to review a harpsichordist, a guitarist, or a high-range singer. Frankly, you would rather not, but it's part of the job. If it were left solely to your personal preference, likes or dislikes, you would pan this recitalist. But as a reviewer you must repress your personal inclinations—but not your standards of taste and performance! All your training and experience in judging artistic quality, and standards of programming and performance, come into play. You will appreciate (with your mind, if you wish) the affirmative and negative points of the recital. You may even forget, for the duration of the recital, your personal preference for a different category of musical event.

The same standard applies to the other arts. You may not care for Westerns, either in the movie theater or on television. This does not mean that all Westerns are bad. Should you review a Western, you would judge whether it is a good movie—and a good Western.

So it goes, along the line, in all the arts. Is your personal taste in paintings for the romantics, or for nonobjective art? An art critic must judge such works on their own terms.

Do you insist that all plays today be "relevant"? A comedy, bland by some standards, may make you laugh in spite of yourself.

All his life, a critic must retain an open mind, a respect for the expert practitioner in any field of the performing and creative arts. His own tastes—but not his standards—probably will broaden. When they start to constrict, it is time to retire as a practicing reviewer.

Chapter V

COMPONENTS OF CRITICISM: DIRECT DATA—MATERIAL, FORM, AND WORKMANSHIP

The late Oscar Thompson, in his *Practical Musical Criticism,* refined Calvocoressi's analysis of the components of criticism and noted that the "direct data"—the music itself—can be divided into the three major factors of material, form, and workmanship. We can apply this formula to anything being reviewed: plays, movies, TV documentaries, books, the fine arts, as well as music.

Naturally, the three categories will often, if not always, overlap. And they will vary in degree of importance. The direct data provide the principal basis for appraising the new work of whatever medium. Important factors, however, are the critic himself—the funnel—and, to some degree, the indirect data, which are considered in the next chapter.

Chapter VII gets down to brass tacks on the structure of a review and what to include in it. The particulars, the details, are the bricks and mortar of a criticism. But there must be a general design. What does one look for in any cultural event?

Even more than excellence or lack of merit in the performance itself, a reviewer examines the creative aspects of a new work of art; and he always hopes to find inspiration, originality, freshness, conviction, soundness of structure in anything he writes about. Words, words, words!

We will deal with these words, words, words again as we proceed to the various branches of reviewing. Now we are talking about material, form, and workmanship—fundamental to a new play, an original screenplay or teleplay, a new book or musical composition, a painting or piece of sculpture.

Is the new work inspired, or something less than that? Right away there is a possible overlap. The inspiration may be in the originality of the play's plot or the musical composition, or in its expert craftsmanship.

Does the play (or movie or musical composition or painting) have originality, or does it immediately remind you of an earlier playwright, composer, or artist? If the latter, the older artisan was probably—but not necessarily—better. Here, too, the critic's experience and abilities to make comparisons come into play.

The new writer or composer may have used a previous practitioner's idea, or structure, and given it a new twist. He may thus bring freshness of treatment to the work. (Fellows named Shakespeare and Bach did that.) In this case, workmanship may be the principal factor for examination.

Whether new or old, is the playwright or composer convincing in what he says (material) and how he says it (workmanship)? This is differentiated from the performance itself, subject of other chapters.

The creative artist may have a good idea (material), but may not have developed it to its fullest extent (workmanship). Or he may take a wisp of a plot and make a frothy comedy out of it.

Again, he may have a good play idea, the plot may teem with possibilities, yet the overall structure may not take advantage of all the material. Or the plot may be top-heavy with subplots that impede the principal action. Here the imbalance of material and form makes a faulty structure.

If it is a new musical show, how do the elements fit? Do the songs and dances further the progress of the libretto, or do they impede it? Is there too much "book" that gets in the way of the songs and dances?

Judgment of a new musical composition, of course, also employs standards of material, form, and workmanship. Does the music have basic worth? Is there sufficient thematic structure? Are the themes developed ably? Or is there too much thematic material to be developed properly within the scope of the composition?

In discussing the material and workmanship, form sometimes is crowded out, but it, too, should be considered. Form may be only a label. That is, a play may be advertised as a comedy and turn out to be a drama. Everyone knows that an opera would never succeed on an eight-performances-a-week basis in a Broadway theater. One of Gian-Carlo Menotti's operas, deemed suitable for theater performance, was termed a musical play. *Maria Golovin* was given on Broadway, but it was (and is) still an opera.

A play with music, musical comedy, musical drama, operetta, light opera, comedy, farce, satire, adventure, fantasy, drama, tragedy, survey, documentary, debate, fiction, nonfiction, symphony, suite, tone poem, rhapsody, concerto, sinfonia concertante—these and other terms may describe the form of the creation being reviewed, and the critic may agree with this label or not.

One may accept a label as to form even though the technical qualifications are not always met. Purists object that Chopin's "Funeral March" sonata is not written in the sonata form, therefore it is not a sonata. To call it a "suite" might be technically appropriate but unjust to the composer's wishes.

The element of form—the firmness of structure, or lack of it—also overlaps into material and workmanship. Some indirect data may have a bearing on form. Woody Allen said his comedy *Don't Drink the Water* was inspired by newspaper headlines of travelers accused as spies in Russia. Critics concentrated on the point that the popular comedy was more a collection of wisecracks than a play. Form, again.

The basic worth of the material of a play may be appraised in terms of universality. Could the setting of the play be transferred to another time or place with equal effect? Several of Shakespeare's plays—*Hamlet, Julius Caesar,* and others—have been given in modern dress. Verdi's *Masked Ball,* transferred for its premiere to a "Colonial Boston" setting because the censor objected to its treatment of the actual assassination of a Swedish king—has since been given in the Boston setting, in an Italian setting, and in its true Swedish locale, and in various time periods from eighteenth century to contemporary.

Come Blow Your Horn, a stage comedy hit about a Jewish family, was changed to concern an Italian family in its movie version. Playgoers of various ethnic backgrounds were heard to remark, "This could be about my family!" The quality of universality aids any creative work.

Has the composer a style of his own, or is he recognizably in debt to Bach, Mozart, Chopin, Wagner, or Debussy? Playwrights may or may not be influenced by Eugene O'Neill, Tennessee Williams, Edward Albee, or their predecessors, and novelists by Hemingway, Joyce, Faulkner, and so on in any of the arts forms. The point is that creative artists who break new ground are not accused of imitating anyone else, although contemporary critics who may not understand their work may castigate them.

In every art form, the truly creative artist has been lambasted. Creative artists find that certain rules of procedure work, said Calvocoressi, but other creative artists may evolve new rules. Do not let rules become recipes. Works criticized for lack of form may actually be breaking new ground. Some of the giants named above, and other originators in the fine arts, were prime targets of this kind of criticism.

Remember Aristotle's "law of dramatic unity"—that all the action of a play must spring from one source and occur in one place within a time span equal to the length of performance? The time unity was later expanded to twenty-four hours. Where would the art of the drama be if these unities were still adhered to?

A critic may ponder that a square peg may be ill at ease in a round hole. He may remark that a full-length play has only enough material for one act, or would have more impact in the shorter form. On the other hand, a one-act play may be so bursting with viable material that it could be expanded profitably to a full-length drama. Such expansions and contractions are made frequently during transfer between stage and television. Prime source for such critical ponderings is the material involved, but form and workmanship matter, too.

The reviewer must always be on guard when a virtuoso is performing a new work: Does the new work succeed (or fail) because of (or in spite of) its creative qualities or because of the caliber of the performance? Or is a show more, or less, worth hearing or seeing, because of its leading actors? A virtuoso musician may make a piece of music sound better than its intrinsic worth. Would this new piece of music still be impressive, although perhaps not so impressive, in the hands of a less brilliant performer?

Many a stage show has been put on as a "vehicle" for a star.

Consider the musical shows in recent years presumably tailored to the talents of Carol Channing, Gwen Verdon, and Barbra Streisand (*Gentlemen Prefer Blondes, Redhead* and *Sweet Charity,* and *Funny Girl.* And where is this "equal rights for men"?!). When the star had to leave the show, it sometimes folded.

In years further back, Alfred Lunt and Lynn Fontanne more than once starred in comedies that never would have succeeded without farceurs of their caliber. Katharine Cornell, who for many years was the epitome of the stage star, won fame for her virtuoso performance in *The Green Hat,* a meretricious play based on a meretricious book by Michael Arlen. Here, as elsewhere, quality of performance can override deficiency in the work performed.

A critic of taste and experience may object to some stage shows and films as "commercial" creations, written to formula, certain treatment or ingredients being included with an eye to mass appeal. (The Hebrew wedding scene in the movie *Thoroughly Modern Millie* was called irrelevant and put there only to attract Jewish patrons.) Pure artistry or creativity may be lessened to assure greater box-office return. The reviewer may voice such objections while at the same time admiring the craftsmanship that fashions the commercial success.

There is, of course, no reason why the commercial and the artistic cannot go hand in hand. *Room Service, Hellzapoppin, Three Men on a Horse,* and *Twelfth Night* were commercial.

"When you get down to it," said Henry T. Murdock, late drama critic of *The Philadelphia Inquirer,* "Eugene O'Neill, S. N. Behrman, Robert E. Sherwood, Elmer Rice, George Kelly, and Sidney Howard were 'commercial.' In their period, 1923–40, they hit the box office, and no one can deny their artistry or their sense of entertainment values. They made the nearest thing to a golden age of our theatre."

Oklahoma!, based on Lynn Riggs's indigenous American play *Green Grow the Lilacs,* changed the character of the Broadway musical stage. Up to March 31, 1943 (the night *Oklahoma!* bowed in New York), few American musicals bothered too much about "book" or "plot." They were mostly to entertain "the tired businessman." Songs, dances, and skits were there whether the show was frankly a revue or not.

Oklahoma! not only gave impetus to the "book" musical—one with a viable libretto—but also introduced ballet (not merely an ensemble of girls' legs kicking); for some years no musical show was complete without a ballet.

Here and elsewhere, we talk about the total effect and how every aspect of a work of art contributes to or detracts from it. In analyzing the vegetable soup, the connoisseur assays the proportion of ingredients and the soup's preparation. He may speculate—mentally, if not in print—on how the soup would have tasted with more or less of one or more ingredients. But the total effect is what matters.

Rarely has a musical show such as *Brigadoon* come along in which all elements—story, music, choreography, decor—have been so unified. This show was all of a piece.

That same season (1947–48) brought *Finian's Rainbow,* a musical whose originality, humor, and philosophy have kept it worth reviving periodically despite the fact that its social satire has been blunted by the passing years.

While on the subject of stage plays and musicals, one should also note the factor of whether a show is brand new, an established hit, or a revival (more of this in Chapter X).

The show may be having its premiere. It may be "trying out" in Philadelphia, Boston, or another city, "en route to Broadway." The critic must judge the show as he sees it, the performance that is in front of him now. He may well speculate—again, mentally or in print—that certain changes might improve the show, might give it a better chance for success on Broadway. But he is not a play doctor, and he is not expected to offer a detailed prescription. His comments, although negative, may still serve as "constructive criticism."

In a musical composition, what is the proportion of material to workmanship? Some questions in this regard were asked earlier in this chapter.

How about a set of variations? Beethoven took an innocuous tune by a little-known composer named Diabelli and put it in the form of a magnificent set of thirty-three variations. You might say the material was practically nothing, the workmanship everything, but this would be splitting hairs. It's the final composition that counts.

A play or book may be virtually unrecognizable from the movie on which it is based. (You recall the author who said he was writing a new novel based on the movie made from his previous novel!) An orchestral transcription of a keyboard work may be, for practical purposes, a new composition. Stokowski's transcriptions of Bach's organ music, notably the *Passacaglia* and the *Toccata and Fugue in D minor,* and Ravel's transcription of Mussorgsky's *Pictures at an Exhibition,* which was a landmark in piano composition, are examples of works that widened the horizon of the originals as well as making them available for orchestral audiences.

Transcriptions of music and plays into other media often reveal as much creativity by the transcriber as by the original writer. The dividing lines of credit may be blurred.

Analysis of material, form, and workmanship is suggested as an aid to the reviewer. After some practice, such appraisal will become subconscious or second nature. The critic will strive to appraise the basic worth of any new work—whether it has genuine substance or is of the fashion of the day, whether there is sound workmanship or merely a high technical finish.

Chapter VI

COMPONENTS OF CRITICISM: INDIRECT DATA

If direct data stem solely from the creative work itself, indirect data are everything external about the work—the author's intentions, expressed, disavowed, or not expressed at all; the work's place in the writer's output, and otherwise in its contemporary setting or place in history; whether the work has any biographical or autobiographical significance, or—in music—any programmatic intent.

Such indirect data—especially concerning a play with some real-life overtones—must be considered. They may have a bearing on what you include in your review, and may even influence your judgment. Often the indirect data can be misleading, as we shall see.

First of all, there is a label of the author himself. Suppose you were seeing a play and didn't know (at the time you were seeing it) who wrote it. You would be forced to base your judgment entirely on the merit of the play itself (an unfair task?!). Later, you find the play was written by an unknown playwright, and is his first play; or the author is Tennessee Williams, or Edward Albee, or Arthur Miller. Would it make any difference in your judgment? (It shouldn't.) It would still be a good, mediocre, or bad play.

One can but admire the scholarship that seeks to ascertain the true composers of works attributed to Vivaldi, Bach, Mozart, and other greats. Some say that the *Eight Little Preludes and Fugues* were written by someone other than Bach. Works written by Vivaldi are still being discovered in the archives of Italian libraries. Are these musical compositions greater or less great for having been written by Bach, Vivaldi, or some other composer?

Whether Shakespeare, Bacon, or somebody else deserves the title of the Bard, do the Bard's plays differ in merit because someone possibly other than a man named Shakespeare wrote some or all of them? In criticizing the *Odyssey,* would it—should it—make any difference to find that "Homer's works were not written by him but by somebody else bearing the same name"?

The point, of course, is that the name of the author should not predispose the critic. Each work should be judged solely on its own merit—and sometimes this is hard!

When reviewing a new artistic work by a prominent creator, it is valid to appraise it in terms of the man's previous output, but only as an aid, not to mislead or to be an end in itself. To call a Shakespeare play or a Beethoven symphony his worst would not necessarily appraise it as bad. To say the product of a hack writer is his best effort is still not saying whether it is good.

Then there is the chronology of the creator's output. To say that something is representative of the composer's early style, when he wrote it late in life, would be misleading—downright wrong, in fact! It could resemble his early style. Would that make a difference in its quality?

The previous chapter mentioned individuality of style versus being in debt to an earlier creative artist. This is one time (among many!) when direct and indirect data are intertwined.

A play may be a good drama, a book may be an excellent novel, a musical composition may impress with its solidity of structure and material. Direct data give you this impression. But if from your background and experience you know that the play, novel, or musical work is in the style of, say, Williams, Hemingway, or Prokofiev, it will have a great bearing on your review. You may praise the craftsmanship and, doubtless, the material, but the indirect data of which you have knowledge prevent you from calling the work's style original.

In reviewing plays or movies (or books), the indirect data can be helpful, or otherwise.

First, does the play have any true-life connections or connotations? ('Djever notice that the screen credits, sometimes even of a biographical movie, include in small letters "The characters herein are fictional, and any resemblance to persons living or dead is coincidental"?) If the play is an avowed biography, how true to life does it appear to be? Has the biographical order of events been followed faithfully, or have they been juggled; have characters and/or events been added or omitted—added for dramatic effect, omitted to avoid cluttering the script?

All this is interesting as to factual accuracy. But it is important to consider whether the tampering with biographical facts enhances or detracts from the quality of the play or movie as a show. Would it be a better (or worse) play or movie if no dramatic license were taken? (Chapter XII deals with the transfer of one story or show to another medium, as from book to play or movie.)

Biographical movies are prime targets of reviewers. Yet who among the living can tell if Paul Muni was the facsimile of Louis Pasteur, Edward G. Robinson the real Dr. Paul Ehrlich, or Don Ameche a true Alexander Graham Bell? How accurately did Montgomery Clift portray Sigmund Freud; Jason Robards, F. Scott Fitzgerald; or Robert Alda, George Gershwin?

On the other hand there is what might be termed fictional biography. Does one really know that Elizabeth Barrett and Robert Browning were the romantics they appeared to be in *The Barretts of Wimpole Street*?

The "romantic interest" often inserted in biographical, usually musical, movies is a prime example of "adjustments" made in a life story. It is always best for a reviewer to check basic sources for facts, biographical or otherwise, rather than rely on statements of producers, press agents, or even the authors.

Quite different from an avowedly biographical show is one in which the author disclaims any real-life basis but which is generally thought otherwise. An outstanding recent example is Arthur Miller's drama *After the Fall,* which everyone except the playwright said concerned his marriage to Marilyn Monroe. Certainly the biographical aspect was of interest. But did it make the play any better or worse?

There is also the show "tailored to the talents of a particular star." This is often true in a musical. But it may not be true at all. A pair of playwrights said of their minor Broadway hit that it had been written with the star in mind (variation: "written for Allen Blank"). Actually, the play had first been written, then cast; the star was the sixth one asked to play the role. A point of interest. But did it affect the quality of the play?

Music is full of examples of indirect data, avowed and disavowed.

First of all, there is program music—music with a title, that tries to tell a story, in contrast to pure music, which is solely for its own sake. But let us take program music on its own terms, for the sake of example.

This is music that has a title and expresses something in general terms: *Prelude to the Afternoon of a Faun, The Seasons, Fingal's Cave Overture.* They may be inspired by a natural phenomenon or a poem. Other program music will try to depict a specific story or things—*Pictures at an Exhibition, The Sorcerer's Apprentice, Till Eulenspiegel's Merry Pranks, Pastoral Symphony.* You can enjoy the music without reading beforehand what the music is supposed to say. Your knowledge of the story or the picture may enhance your enjoyment of the music—but does it make the music itself any greater?

Sometimes it may be better not to know the author's intentions. A recent composition by a Philadelphia composer was premiered by the Philadelphia Orchestra. The music itself was not bad—it had body and drama. But the program notes gave detailed exposition of the composer's intentions—to depict the Creation—and the music fell so far short of this that an overall negative impression was gained, whereas without the program notes the impression would have been positive. Here was an example in which the music, as music only, was effective, but taken in the larger context of what the composer tried to accomplish, it failed. (Some people should quit while they're ahead!)

Many times musicologists profess to find extramusical qualities in a composer's writing, qualities just as often flatly denied by the composer. Mahler, for one, disclaimed biographical inspiration in some of his symphonies, but musical commentators insist it is there. Others, creative artists themselves, find that a musical composition conjures a certain mental picture and give it an unwelcome but lasting nickname. Beethoven's publisher, to help sales, dubbed it the *Moonlight Sonata,* for instance. This of course has no bearing on the quality of the music.

Words of press agents and producers should be heard with caution. A wary eye is recommended for composers, too.

Composers of other eras often used part of one composition in a later work. Bach used various themes in many forms, Handel often transposed an aria from one opera to another. It was an accepted practice then. But it would be a mistake for a reviewer to comment how appositely the "Soldiers' Chorus" fits into *Faust* without knowing that Gounod had written this stirring piece of music for an earlier work that failed, so why not put it to good use?

Commentators love to write about the inspiration for great musical works. There was speculation as to whether Richard Wagner wrote *Tristan and Isolde* because he was in love with Mathilde Wesendonck or whether he was in love with Mathilde Wesendonck because he was writing *Tristan.*

Sometimes the extramusical writings of composers themselves are as inspired as their music. Consider Berlioz' description of how he wrote "The March to the Scaffold" from his *Symphonie Fantastique.* He avowed that he composed it in a few hours, "in a night of fever" when he roved fields of snow while Chopin and Liszt sought his body at the Paris morgue.

This romantic statement was accepted for half a century until one musicologist found that the march was part of an earlier opera, *Les Francs-Juges,* and was inserted into the *Symphonie* score with no alteration except the addition of four measures.

To sum up—indirect data can be helpful and/or misleading. To be acquainted with an author's previous works may be necessary, yet may prejudice the reviewer. An interview with a creative artist, concerning his intentions, may make the critic an unwitting apologist for the writer. The path of objectivity is sometimes hard to tread.

Chapter VII

GENERAL STRUCTURE OF A PLAY REVIEW

These suggestions on the structure of a review are meant as guidelines, not as a straitjacket. There is no wish to stifle the creativity of any critic. But even as one must walk before one can run, the beginning reviewer may welcome a set of rules that, later, he may feel at liberty to ignore—provided he writes intelligibly and convincingly.

As mentioned earlier, an arts review is not written in the strict inverted-pyramid form so that it may be trimmed from the end as necessary. The trimming may be done that way (usually to the reviewer's embarrassment or chagrin); sometimes a review may be written that way. But for the present, let us assume not.

Instead, if an architectural form is needed, use a column topped by part of an inverted pyramid, and resting on a pyramid base. The inverted-pyramid top is, of course, an attention-getting lead—desired in any article in the newspaper. The main body of your review (the "column") will detail the nature of the show, a minimum of synopsis, appraisal of individual performances and consideration of such technical credits as writing, direction, and decor. The conclusion—the base of the pyramid—will be a wrap-up comment.

The first paragraph or two will summarize your impression of the play. Just as types of news leads in basic reporting are varied, the leads on show reviews are equally diverse.

An ordinary "Five W's" lead might read like this:

"Cotton Candy, a comedy as light and tasty as its title, had its premiere last night at the Forrest. Or: *"Cotton Candy,* a comedy that belies the lightness of its title, opened last night" . . .

If you are not prepared to give a firm thumbs-up or thumbs-down verdict in your first sentence, a straight news-story lead would read: *"Cotton Candy,* a comedy by Candace Cotten, had its premiere at the Playhouse last night."

Another form of lead starts with a generality and gets specific:
"A decade ago the Western began its long reign on television. Five years ago situation comedies started a trend. The forerunner in what appears to be television's latest cycle bowed on ABC last night. Its title: 'Bewitched.'"

You could turn this around, thus: " 'Bewitched,' the forerunner in what is sure to be television's newest cycle, succeeding comedies and Westerns, bowed last night on ABC."

Then there is the shocker, inspired by an exceptional show. "The musical of the century" was Brooks Atkinson's appraisal of *My Fair Lady*. "*Saratoga* is a great big bore" was how a Philadelphia reviewer initially characterized a highly touted expensive musical.

The "where" and "when" of a review are not so important as these two W's would be in an accident story. But somewhere in the first paragraph or two you should name the theater (for a movie having a "saturation" opening, it may be "area theaters"). It is not strictly necessary to say when the show opened; "at the Rialto" may suffice.

Early in the article, although not necessarily in the first sentence, should be a capsule description of the play and, if possible, your verdict. "A frothy comedy that bubbles all the way"; "A comedy that succeeds, despite its light weight, because of superior performances"; or "A lightweight comedy whose deft performers cannot overcome its weaknesses."

The pluses and the minuses of a new show may be so balanced that you cannot reach a clear-cut decision. In that case, your review will reflect this. If full consideration of all the factors leads to indecision, by all means stay on the fence. However, stay on the fence only as a last resort; habitual fence-sitters have few readers. Come to a favorable or unfavorable conclusion whenever you can; the reader expects it of you. If he doesn't get it, he is disappointed. Sometimes you will disappoint the reader who depends on your verdict as a guide to whether he should spend money for that show. But you should maintain a good batting average.

Somewhere by the second or third paragraph you will have named the author or authors. If the playwright is famous, his name may suffice. If not, you may want to add a phrase or two—"first play by George Spelvin, author of many movie and television scripts," or "by George Spelvin, whose only previous produced play was the comedy, *Kisses and Misses,* two years ago." Next, convey to the reader the nature of the show and how well the playwright succeeds in the qualities of perception and writing.

Does the plot have universality? Is the story believable? Are the characters drawn true to life or in caricature? Are the characters humanly etched or are they all black or all white (we are not speaking racially here)? Is the plot well drawn, is it taut, or does the playwright leave loose ends? Are all the characters in proportion to their pre-

Perhaps the most famous role portrayed by Helen Hayes, longtime First Lady of the Theater, was that of Queen Victoria in *Victoria Regina,* in which she "aged" sixty years during the course of the play.

(NBC TELEVISION PHOTO)

sumed importance in the play, or does one or more seem to be around too much or too little, considering his importance to the story?

Does the playwright write with insight? Does he dip beneath the surface in plot construction and character analysis? Does the drama or comedy move forward steadily, or is it uneven in pace? Are there interruptions—digressions or unnecessary characters—that serve only to pad out the story?

Another important factor often enters the appraisal: Does the play have a message?

A message is perfectly acceptable in a play. In fact, if the play does not convey some message or moral, expressed or inherent, it is liable to be dull. However, the play is the thing, not the message.

When the play, fictional or not, has a message, the reviewer should be careful to check his own feelings. He may strongly agree or disagree with the author's precepts. Whether the author is right or wrong in what he is saying, the important thing is: How well does he say it, in terms of a good play? Any experienced reviewer has had to sit through at least two acts of a stage presentation that was more sermon or diatribe than play.

Sunrise at Campobello dramatized Franklin D. Roosevelt's contracting of poliomyelitis and touched on his early political life. Republican and Democratic critics praised its dramatic impact. But one die-hard Republican stormed out of the theater, calling the drama "arrant political nonsense." He should have checked his political beliefs at the door.

This is not to suggest that a reviewer should not have feelings about any controversial or noncontroversial subject. (Reviewers, some people insist, are human.) But he does not lose his head when he writes his review.

All comment on the nature of the play should back up your initial characterization of the show in your first or second paragraph.

Now you are ready to describe the plot. But keep the synopsis to a minimum. Tell only enough to give the reader an idea of what's going on. Avoid inning-by-inning detail.

As an example of general description versus inning-by-inning, take the course at Temple University, which is entitled, rather formally, "Reviewing and Critical Writing." I describe it as "making expert theater and music reviewers in thirty easy lessons." Adding detail, I state that students are told the general structure of reviews, what to look and listen for, and are given some practical tips on journalistic writing; also what to avoid.

This, I hope, is better than telling someone, "The first period we discuss the nature of criticism, the second week I tell them the structure of a theater review, the third week we talk about a solo recital," and so on. Thrilling, eh?

Thus by avoiding the inning-by-inning version of the synopsis, you also round out your analysis of the play.

Take, for instance, Alan King in a new comedy, *The Impossible Years*. In the first couple of paragraphs you have mentioned the play, playwrights, theater, and star, and capsulized your reaction. Now follows something like this:

"King plays a harassed psychiatrist who is unable to cope with his teenage daughter. Members of the audience, many of whom undoubtedly are in the same predicament, laugh frequently at the star's troubles. The play seems tailor-made for the talents of the nightclub comedian, who is making his legitimate stage debut." (You may speculate that the play was written with this star in mind, and find that the authors insist the play came first. Sometimes you will be able to check beforehand.)

"The frustrations continue with hordes of boy friends and rock 'n' roll recordings, the psychiatrist's wife giving what support she can. If this comedy seems like an overgrown TV script, it is because the playwrights are veteran TV and movie scripters, and their latest work seems destined for films."

Note that the paragraphs above give a general idea of the nature. quality, and originality of the script. There is little plain synopsis—perhaps a little more could be added.

Note, too, that except for the star, no character has yet been named. We didn't say "the teenage daughter, played by Charlotte Russo," or "the psychiatrist's wife (or King's wife), played by Betty Belfry." Naming subsidiary characters at this point clutters your writing.

After you have finished summarizing the play, get down to the business of explicit credits. List the players in meritorious order. Although you have mentioned the star in the lead and the synopsis, you may not have described his performance fully. Now is the time.

"King, as the father of a teenage daughter (or two or three or whatever number teenagers), is entirely at home when he is the center of attention, but tends to languish when his stage wife or daughter has the limelight." Or:

"King is entirely at home in the role, and the force of his personality helps gloss over weaknesses in the script." Or:

"Despite a tailor-made script, King's admitted talent for nightclubs or television is insufficient for the greater demands of the legitimate stage. He seems unable to maintain fervor of performance the whole evening."

The above theoretical paragraphs are, of course, only illustrations, and you may well use more space in describing the star's performance.

You now mention any subsidiary characters worth mentioning. When it is a new show, describe the characters played; the stage name means little or nothing. A sentence or descriptive phrase helps fill in chinks from your play description and synopsis earlier:

"Betty Belfry plays the psychiatrist's wife with a combination of frustration and boredom that lends piquancy to her characterization." Or, "Betty Belfry's performance lends distinction to an otherwise stereotyped role as a frustrated mother, the psychiatrist's wife." Or, "Betty Belfry plays the psychiatrist's wife, and her performance unfortunately reflects her frustration as the rebellious teenager's mother."

"Charlotte Russo has the important part of Linda, the teenager. She brings individuality and wins some sympathy in a role that typifies today's teenager."

Or, "Charlotte Russo has the important part of Linda, the teenager herself, but her performance adds nothing to round out the picture of today's rebellious youth."

As the players decrease in importance of role or merit of performance, they are named next. Note that the characterizations are given rather than the characters' stage names:

"Donald White enacts King's psychiatrist colleague, also the father of a teenager, with broad comedy; Jacob Slater makes the most of his bit as a television repairman; Minnie Merton is eloquent as Linda's chum. Giving good support are Curtis Washington as Linda's No. 1 boy friend, Addie Welch as a garrulous maid, and Grace Knapp as a philosophical teacher."

It is unnecessary to give the stage names of these subsidiary characters. It adds little or nothing to say ". . . Dr. Johnson, King's psychiatrist colleague" or ". . . Carol, Linda's chum." On the other hand, merely to mention the stage name is insufficient: ("Curtis Washington as Bob, Addie Welch as Hattie, Grace Knapp as Miss Jones.")

A reminder: When mentioning characters and describing the

synopsis, do not mix your performers and the characters they play.

"Rock Hudson plays a shipwrecked sailor who is cast onto a Pacific island and falls in love with Doris Day." The sailor doesn't fall in love with Doris Day. A similar bad example: "Rock Hudson is shipwrecked onto a desert island and falls in love with a native girl there." No, Rock doesn't. The sailor he plays does.

If the direction, settings, costuming, lighting—any of the technical factors—are outstandingly good or bad, you may have mentioned them earlier in your review. Following your appraisal of the principal performances, here is where you give credit or discredit where due. You may expand on any technical appraisals previously mentioned, or, if they have already been sufficiently discussed, round out your listing of credits.

"Christopher Robinson's direction maintains a steady pace," or "Christopher Robinson's direction never allows the pace to sag," or "Director Christopher Robinson seemed content to let the players go their own lackadaisical ways."

"Joseph Miller's setting of a cluttered living room gives ample visual backing for the goings-on."

Having enumerated the cast and credits, you come to the review-ending pyramid base. When possible, give a further summary of your concise reaction to the show: *"The Impossible Years* are all too probable; the show should be around awhile." "All in all, a show that is funny despite its stereotypes." "Parents of teenagers will love this show. So will any other playgoers with an ounce of sympathy." "Television viewers will love this one."

You may not always be able to think up a concluding pithy statement that doesn't repeat your lead, nor will you always be able to take a forthright stand here. Indeed, a concluding paragraph of this kind is not entirely necessary. But it gives a final and refreshing fillip to your review.

Having given the reader a general impression of thumbs up or thumbs down (or thumbs sideways), do not overturn this impression—in other words, do not contradict yourself—in appraising details.

You may start off by panning a play, but if you highly praise the individual performances, the direction, and the decor, you may confuse the reader. Be sure to give the necessary qualifications: "Although the play is poor, the actors give their all, and director Howard March does his best to overcome the script's handicap."

The same is true if you praise the play but pan the performances, direction, and settings.

In the first case, you might use some phrase such as "the whole does not equal the sum of its parts." In the second instance, "the whole more than equals the sum of its parts."

Chapter VIII

AVANT-GARDE THEATER

All of the foregoing has been written with what may be termed a "traditional" play in mind. How does one deal with the avant-garde, or black comedy, or theater of the absurd, by such playwrights as Harold Pinter or Edward Albee or Arthur Kopit or Israel Horovitz?

These playwrights are the leaders of some sort of revolution, the past decade representing the greatest shift in expression, Henry T. Murdock points out, since the 1920's and 1930's with the emergence of Anderson, Barrie, Coward, O'Neill, Kaufman and Ferber, Kaufman and Connelly, Kaufman and Hart, Lillian Hellman, and Sidney Howard. They bore out the promise of a previous revolution of several decades earlier, with Ibsen, Shaw, Strindberg, Synge and Yeats.

Frankly, the offbeat review is harder to write for the simple reason that the play is harder to understand, and therefore harder to interpret.

To go much further afield, how does a critic appraise theatrical presentations—they are not always called "plays"—by such groups as Julian Beck's Living Theater, the Polish Laboratory Theater, and others in which audience participation is a prime ingredient of the evening? What about the improvisatory productions? How important is the new freedom of language and of dress or undress (nudity) to the total impact of the stage production at hand?

Obviously those productions that seek audience participation have a purpose, although the message may not always be clear. And their efforts to involve the audience may backfire; either the members of the audience clam up, or, if the audience participation takes an unexpected turn, the actor is discomfited or nonplussed.

Where are the critic's standards to be applied here? What provides his basis for evaluation of play content and performance? The standards dealt with in the preceding chapter may be applied in part, but certainly not in toto. To say that the critic must develop his own standards to fit each individual case is stating the case perhaps a bit too simply.

We have mentioned plays with a message and cautioned the reviewer to judge the play as such, whether or not he agrees with the message. The same caution should apply here. Should the reviewer "get involved," should he be one of the audience participants? Would the production be more meaningful for him if he participated? Would his review be more meaningful if he participated? Is his

Samuel Beckett's *Waiting for Godot* was one of the first avant-garde plays. Bert Lahr, long famous as a comedian, won new laurels in the role of Vladimir.

(UPI PHOTO)

primary obligation to be objective? Can his review be as valid if he is entirely objective, or might he be missing something?

A categorical answer cannot be given here. My own experience over the years would steer me toward objectivity, toward observing the audience participation and the effect of the evening as a whole, as a reporter, not as a participant. But this may be the generation gap!

However, one suggestion from an earlier chapter may be recalled and broadened. If a critic's tastes harden, it's time for him to leave the reviewing field. Similarly, he must ever retain flexibility in judging the theater of the twenty-first century.

Chapter IX

REVIEWING MOVIES

The recipe for the basic structure of a play review applies to movies as well. There is a principal additional factor—the use of the camera. The screen is two-dimensional, the stage is three-dimensional, but astute camera work can more than make up the difference.

Not only can the camera roam beyond the confines of a stage, whether proscenium or arena, but all sorts of "trick" and special effects are possible. The split-second flashbacks in the memory of *The Pawnbroker* were hailed as a milestone in the art of film-making. Movies by Ingmar Bergman and other masters of the cinematic art use the camera creatively.

Here, too, in his conscious or subconscious analysis of a movie, the reviewer will assay the camera work in the whole pattern. Is the trick photography a substitute for substance, or does it enhance the story? Does it help carry the action along or is it merely obtrusive? In other words, are the special effects necessary to the story or merely a gimmick?

The breathtaking, panoramic view (in full color) of the Austrian Alps that opened the movie *The Sound of Music* may have had little or nothing to do with the story. It certainly was not a part of the stage production. But it immediately put the moviegoer in a strongly receptive mood. The imaginative camera work was undoubtedly a major factor—along with the appeal of the story, the songs, and the many children in the cast—in attracting thousands of persons to see this movie more than once, sometimes many times.

The motion picture camera, being even more mobile than the human eye, can achieve effects impossible in a live stage production. Such mobility has been put to good use by the impressionists and makers of "underground" movies.

Some movies are made with a specific audience in mind. Some may

Rex Harrison, who originated the role of Professor Enry 'Iggins in *My Fair Lady,* is seen here with Audrey Hepburn, who played Eliza in the film version. Miss Hepburn was chosen because Julie Andrews, who starred on the stage, "wasn't big enough box-office" for the movies—at the time.

appeal primarily to college students, to people with a particular interest or to members of one race. It would be well if the reviewer could attempt to see the movie from the viewpoint of the group for which it is primarily intended. But if he is writing for a newspaper of general circulation (not a specialized periodical), he will appraise the picture in general terms while still mentioning its specialized appeal.

Both white and black movie producers in the early 1970's suddenly discovered that Negroes are a sizable portion of the theater audience and are worth catering to—speaking in terms of number of tickets sold. The first "black" movies were frankly racist—*Shaft* and *Shaft's Big Score* are but two examples—in which the blacks were the goodies and Whitey was the baddie.

But soon some intrinsically better movies, geared to the "black" market, appeared, and because they had a quality of universality, they appealed to the "white" market as well. *Sounder* is an example.

When this was written the freedom from censorship was relatively new, and nudity was rampant—sometimes quite attractively so!—on both stage and screen. *Oh, Calcutta!* was the prime stage example, preceded by the less startling but more durable rock musical *Hair*.

Any adult who attended movies in the early '70s—the decade, not his age—probably saw some in which nudity was an important part of the camera work. Indeed, several motion pictures were made as frank instruction in the art of sex, ostensibly for married couples. Others got in as much nudity as then possible and built a story around it. Some, such as *Camille 2000,* updated an older story (Dumas' *Lady of the Camellias* or *La Traviata*).

The better movies use snatches of nudity where it is logically a part of the story, with no particular emphasis on the beauties of the human body as such. As the novelty of nudity wears off, this will be more the case in stage shows as well as movies. It is up to the reviewer to decide whether the nude scenes are properly a part of the story, whether they are tastefully done or merely inserted for sensationalism.

Most of all, the critic will assay the movie on all its points—plot, characterization, technical effects or material, form, and workmanship—in terms of the cinematic medium. Is it a good motion picture or could it be played on the stage with little change?

*   *   *

This review by Lynn Martin, a 1967 student at Temple University, leaves no doubt as to her opinion. The ending, burlesquing travelogues, gives a surprise and an amusing fillip. Note that there is practically no synopsis, but rather a general picture of the movie's characteristics. Nor are the actors and the characters they play mixed up. Although the reviewer found one or two favorable points, they by no means outweigh her main premise.

About as unorganized and insignificant as its theme, the motion picture, "Sand Pebbles," has the one redeeming quality of Steve McQueen doing a good job as Jake Holman, a ship's rebellious engine man. The movie opened at neighborhood theaters Wednesday.

Based on a play by Robert Anderson and produced by Robert Wise, "Sand Pebbles" is a conglomeration of scenes which are exciting for excitement's sake. Named from the American gunboat San Pablo stationed off China's coast in 1926, the movie drifts along aimlessly like the boat which is supposed to protect U.S. missionaries.

Trite themes like near-mutiny of the crew, an interracial marriage, American flag-waving, the evils of prostitution, a man's stubborn blindness to love—these are just a few—are coupled with dreadful acting to make the movie as rusty as the ship.

Leading this list is Candice Bergen, who plays the part of an American schoolteacher who brazenly proposes to Holman. Her quivering lips—or maybe it's the weak plot—send him back to his only love, his engines.

Despite the unbelievable character, McQueen plays the emotionless part with the necessary, restrained skill. Another plus is the delightful, romantic musical theme.

But these two highlights are overshadowed by scenes which describe too pictorially an execution, a battle, and a boxing match just for their shock value.

As the San Pablo floats slowly into the blurry, poorly colored sunset, it should sink.

This review is not perfect—there are one or two trite phrases and one or two technical omissions. The director is not named (it's Robert Wise), and since the musical theme is mentioned, its composer should be credited. But the review is compact and witty.

* * *

This review, by a student in the same class, has too much synopsis and mixes the players and characters. The use of parentheses is distracting to the reader. The final sentence refers to "a topic not usually presented," but the reader is not sure what the topic is.

"The Sand Pebbles," starring Steve McQueen, is a movie which kept the audience at the Cheltenham Theater sitting on the edge of their seats, cheering, booing, and gasping at the vivid scenes before them.

Robert Anderson's gripping screenplay, based on Richard McKenna's novel, tells the dramatic story about Americans caught in the turbulence of China in the 20's.

Jake Holman (McQueen), an American sailor, arrives in China for assignment aboard the gunboat, San Pablo. Having given up making peace with the world, Holman just wants adventure without responsibility. However, he cannot accept the way the boat is being run by Captain Collins (Richard Crenna), or the reasons for the gunboat's very existence.

Romantic interest is offered by Shirley Eckart (Candice Bergen), a young American schoolteacher who has come to China to work at a mission. The poignant relationship between Frenchy (Richard Attenborough), an American sailor, and Maily (Marayat Andriane), his Chinese bride, points out the frustration of naval regulations. Frenchy performs his own marriage ceremony when the rite is forbidden by his superiors.

McQueen is outstanding as the expatriate sailor who finally realizes that he cannot be a machine and remain a man.

Attenborough, who has the compassionate part of Frenchy, wins the sympathy and respect of the audience by his quiet, but resolute performance.

The captain (Crenna) seems to be more insane, than representative of the blindness of rigid military regimen.

Miss Bergen, as the schoolteacher, is unable to bring her role to life. Instead, she seems miserably lost to a saccharine part.

Marayat Andriane, who makes her professional debut in "The Sand Pebbles," does not say much, but is able to transmit her role of Maily with sensitivity. Mrs. Andriane is the wife of SEATO's director of administration.

Mako, although his is not a major role, steals the scene more than once with his ability to convey sensitivity as well as strength. He plays the part of a coolie on board the San Pablo who teaches Holman what self-respect means.

Although there are some weak spots in the script and Robert Wise's direction, "The Sand Pebbles" is a formidable contender for an Academy Award.

This movie is for those who want an action picture done with taste and flair on a topic not usually presented.

Chapter X

MUSICAL COMEDIES

Opera is drama, sometimes comedy, that is sung instead of spoken, and has orchestral accompaniment. Operetta is comedy, sometimes drama, that is mostly sung and generally has some spoken lines. Musical comedy, America's contribution to stage forms, is mostly spoken, and has songs that may further the action or may merely be interpolated (the same applies to operatic arias).

There may or may not be ballet or other forms of dancing in any of these musical productions. There is generally a chorus. In musical comedy, the singing and dancing choruses are often the same.

The same criteria apply to musical productions as apply to spoken plays and movies, except there are more factors to judge and the emphases will vary accordingly. A musical costs more than a straight play or movie. Some recent stage musical productions have approached the million-dollar mark, and despite big names as stars, writers, and directors, there is by no means any guarantee that the show will be a hit or even pay off its production costs. When one considers the increasing costs and the increasing financial risks in producing for Broadway, it is a wonder the "fabulous invalid" survives—but it does.

The higher costs are the result of the musical factors and the fact that productions tend to be more lavish. The settings may be grandiose, the technical effects limited only by mechanics and imagination, not by money.

The very elaborateness of musical productions, whether on stage or screen, throws stardust in the reviewer's eyes. He may be dazzled by the spectacle, or the virtuosity of the leading performers. These, of course, are pertinent factors in the overall picture. But it is the entire picture that matters.

Previously we have cited the fact that virtuoso performances can outweigh or overcome faulty creativity. Nowhere is this more applicable than in musicals on stage or screen that are "vehicles" for a star. A musical starring Barbra Streisand or Julie Andrews is almost (note we said "almost") guaranteed to be a hit and make money for its producers, even with a story and songs that might fail with less gifted stars.

The checklist of factors, given earlier for plays and movies, applies here with some additions. Besides story values, performances, direction, and decor, there are the musical elements—the words and music of the songs, and the choreography.

Success begets success. Sometimes a play is turned into a musical. But *Lorelei* is another musical based on the musical comedy *Gentlemen Prefer Blondes,* which made Carol Channing a star. Here she is seen in the title role of *Hello, Dolly!,* which broke the Broadway record of *My Fair Lady* and then was outdistanced by *Fiddler on the Roof.*

The story is generally simpler than that of a straight play or movie, because songs and dances take time. But of course they should do more than take up space. Do the songs and dances fit in; are they a piece with the rest of the show? Do they enhance a libretto or get in its way? A "book" may discreetly take a subsidiary position when songs and dances come along. How unified and well balanced is this musical show, and how much does this balance, or lack of it, affect the overall merit of the show?

Are the songs catchy, the kind you can hum when leaving the theater? Are the lyrics clever? Does the show succeed or fail because of, or in spite of, its songs, libretto, settings, dances, or individual performers? The critic may write that "the songs give the book a much-needed lift" or "the songs do nothing to relieve the tedium of the libretto."

Incidentally, do the songs come across—can you understand the words? Musical comedians' diction is usually clearer than that of opera singers, for example. On the theater stage or in movies, enunciation of the words matters more than the actual singing voice. Sometimes a star cannot sing, but can carry off his part anyhow by virtual parlando—speaking the words in the songs. An outstanding example is the role of Professor Higgins in *My Fair Lady,* from Rex Harrison on.

A performer may achieve stardom via a show that seems tailored to his or her talents. The show may have been written with this star in mind, such as Gwen Verdon or Sammy Davis, Jr., or it may have benefited by exceptionally fortunate casting. The reviewer may ponder on how much of the show's success is owed to the writing, direction, and decor, and how much is because of the star's impact. The star's performance may be so incandescent that the critic need not ponder much or long.

On the other hand, few theatrical experiences are as dreary as a stage or screen musical that just doesn't come off, when the songs and story are leadweighted and so are the stars and dancers. With a musical even more than with a straight play, the show is liable to be a hit or a flop. The verdict is rarely fifty-fifty.

Chapter XI

NEW PLAY VERSUS OLD PLAY: HOW THE REVIEWS DIFFER; OPERETTAS

The principal difference between reviews of new and old shows is simple. In the new play, you concentrate on the show itself, how convincing it is, how original. In an old show, the play itself is mentioned more or less briefly, and you give more attention to the performances.

It depends how familiar the show is. With *Hamlet* or *Carmen,* for instance, you write almost entirely about the performers and very little about the "book." To give a synopsis of either would insult the intelligence of your readers.

Yet there are bound to be some readers who do not know the story of *Hamlet* or *Carmen*. So you give a tactful idea here and there. You may do it in appraising the portrayal of the title role and lesser roles, too.

"John Player gives a virile, striking portrayal of the Danish prince who has difficulty making up his mind to avenge his father's murder." "John Player is convincingly vacillating as the Danish prince sworn to avenge his father's murder." "The production is lackluster because John Player is colorless in the all-important role of the prince sworn to avenge his father's murder."

"Like many operas, a production of *Carmen* can stand or fall with the central character. Nellie Rank brought the production to life with her sexy, spitfire portrayal of the gypsy girl who loves with abandon."

"Otherwise admirable, this production of *Carmen* almost collapsed because of the vocal and visual inadequacies of Nellie Rank in the title role. Her portrayal of the gypsy girl whose romantic capriciousness brings death was more like a middle-aged schoolteacher than a hip-swinging young spitfire."

Of course, you need not limit yourself to a sentence or two in discussing enactments of famous roles.

James Ray (left) and Richard Kiley in a scene from Molière's *Tartuffe,* presented by the Philadelphia Drama Guild at the city's historic Walnut Street Theater. The Drama Guild, headed by a dentist (Dr. Sidney Bloom) who is a theater buff, presents revivals of the classics and recent Broadway hits, with Equity casts headed by leading actors, to supplement Philadelphia's sometimes meager Broadway offerings.

You may choose to compare this performance with previous ones you have seen or heard. This is permissible when it enhances your present description, but ordinarily you accentuate the positive—concentrate on the qualities of the present performer. "Mme. Ponderosa sang Brünnhilde with a tonal opulence reminiscent of Flagstad," or "that did not erase memories of Flagstad." You can use such a comparison if you yourself heard Flagstad. Whether or not you heard Flagstad, a phrase omitting this legendary soprano's name may serve as well: "Mme. Ponderosa sang Brünnhilde with overpowering tonal opulence," or "Mme. Ponderosa's Brünnhilde had tonal power but not the ultimate in opulence."

To digress a bit more: "comparisons are odious," but when you use them, be sure the example is the recognized ultimate, one that the reader can instantly identify. To say "the Phillies played as badly as the Mets on an off day" (prior to 1969!) would mean something; "the Phillies played as badly as the Cardinals on an off day" would not.

In making comparisons of any sort, stay within your own experience. "The best movie of the year" would imply that you have seen them all, poor fellow. "Certainly one of the best movies of the year" or "a sure candidate for an Academy Award" is just as forthright but technically not all-inclusive.

"The most vivid 'Carmen' in memory." If your memory is a long one, fine. If this is but the second time you have seen *Carmen*, better tread carefully.

One also should concentrate on the performance, rather than the play, for the umpteenth production of a recent popular show or a standard opera, such as *Man of La Mancha, The Sound of Music, My Fair Lady, La Bohème, Madame Butterfly,* or *Faust.*

But again, you fill in chinks of the story with a word or two about principal roles as you mention their portrayers. This way you do not offend the reader who knows all about these roles, yet you give a hint to the man who may not know this show.

The revival of a comparatively recent play stands between a new show and a classic. Tennessee Williams' *The Glass Menagerie* is an example. Here you would give major attention to the performance rather than to the description of the play itself, but you also may mention how permanent a drama you think *The Glass Menagerie* is, how well it stands up today.

Comments and occasional comparisons of production details in revivals are also pertinent. The comparisons need not be direct.

"Given in-the-round, with the most elementary of stylized settings, 'My Fair Lady' cast its wonted spell because of its masterful book and songs. . . ."

Occasionally, there are revivals of the ruling American stage form of half a century ago, the operetta. Victor Herbert's *Babes in Toyland, The Red Mill,* and *Naughty Marietta;* Sigmund Romberg's *The Student Prince* and *Blossom Time;* Rudolf Friml's *The Firefly* enjoyed long stage runs and movie careers. They were the product of a less sophisticated day and were a compromise between grand opera and musical comedy.

Their music is less familiar than it was, because they have been largely displaced by shows of Richard Rodgers and Oscar Hammerstein, Irving Berlin, Frank Loesser, Cole Porter, and later writers. Yet there is an occasional summer or amateur revival of the operetta, and audiences are usually taken by the appealing songs and naive story.

Sir John Gielgud, one of Great Britain's most famous and versatile actors, has long been known for his Hamlet. Shown here in a 1936 photograph, Sir John is pictured in the title role of the immortal Shakespeare tragedy.

The reviewer will often treat such a revival for what it is, a period piece. The critic places it in perspective, detailing its virtues and defects as of then and now. The proportion may differ according to date.

Yet for most of the critic's readers (and perhaps the critic himself), the operetta revival may be a new show. Here again, while not insulting the intelligence of his older readers with a lengthy synopsis, he achieves his objective of informing his younger readers through brief, sometimes parenthetical references to the plot.

Gilbert & Sullivan operas (most of them are really operettas) occupy a similar place. *The Mikado, The Pirates of Penzance,* and *H.M.S. Pinafore* may be so familiar to many readers that little plot detail is necessary. Some of the rarely produced G & S shows, however, need more synopsis.

So far as critics and theatregoers are concerned, Gilbert & Sullivan operettas are unique in this respect: You either love 'em or can't stand 'em. (I love 'em.)

The revival of a little-known play is in a special category. It may be a Grecian or Restoration classic. What makes it a classic? Is it worth reviving? Does the present production do justice to the play? Here, too, you may treat the show almost as a new one, in giving the reader an idea of what's going on—*Lysistrata* or *The Country Wife,* but not necessarily *Oedipus Rex.*

The revival of a little-known opera is treated much like a new opera, but the reviewer should try to provide an answer to the obvious question: Why isn't this opera in the repertoire now? Music, libretto, or both? Perhaps it poses great problems of casting or production. The leading role may be so difficult that few singers will essay it.

In any play, new or old, a question to be answered for yourself and your readers is this: Does the play have universality? If the answer is "yes" to a revival, the play is worth reviving. If the answer is "yes" to a new play, such as *Come Blow Your Horn,* the chances are this play will succeed.

A play need not have universality. It may exploit a unique situation successfully. But universality, like charm, is a major plus factor.

Chapter XII

TELEVISION REVIEWING

The criteria used for a movie apply to a drama or comedy on television—freshness and originality of story, quality of acting, direction, and physical production. The last factor includes optimum use of camera and, if warranted, special effects.

Other factors apply in judging documentaries. There are also several points unique to the TV medium.

Unique, for one, is the time straitjacket: The show must generally be given within 15, 30, 60, 90, or 120 minutes, minus time for commercials and station breaks. Movies and stage shows rarely have such a strict time limit.

Sometimes a network will ignore a round-figure length for a show, and fill in with a featurette for the remaining minutes.

The overall TV scene is constantly changing. As with the movies in prior years, the medium is prey to "cycles"—the Western, the situation comedy, the spy story, the supernatural, either in comedy or melodrama, the variety show, and subdivisions of these categories.

The increasing number of "specials," preempting a series program, has altered the pattern of 13, 26, 39 installments of a series. (So have higher production costs; summer reruns start sooner.) And the American Broadcasting Company has experimented with stories having "as many chapters as necessary," with no preconceived number of installments.

Aside from the quality of the show per se, the reviewer should question whether the length is ideal for this presentation. Is it a drama jammed into half an hour or an hour, but which cries for a lengthier production? Is it a wispy comedy spread out over an hour or more, but which deserves much less?

Is it a show that would profit by being presented in installments? Once the National Broadcasting Company presented a "white paper" on American foreign policy that took 3½ hours, the whole evening's "prime time." Reviewers generally praised the idea but were unanimous in suggesting that the program would have been more effective if given in two, three, or four installments.

When ABC presented a four-hour program on Africa, it announced in advance the general subjects of the four hour-long segments, and it rebroadcast these segments on four succeeding days.

By the same token a drama or documentary presented in install-

Westinghouse Broadcasting Company's "Mike Douglas Show" is perhaps the most successful of the daily syndicated variety shows. It originates from KYW-TV in Philadelphia near Independence Hall. Here Douglas is shown (right) in a light moment with Bill Withers, contemporary musical superstar.

ments may have carried more impact if given in one long showing. This may apply to certain lengthy movies that, to accommodate commercials and the time straitjacket, are presented in two television installments on successive evenings.

The movies, both before and since television, have had documentaries—noncartoon short subjects, travelogues, "The March of Time," and full-length features such as *Man of Aran* and *The Plough That Broke the Plains*. But the documentary has reached its fullest flowering in television. It offers the widest scope for the medium and is often a challenge to reviewers.

Here the critic is expected to be a "temporary expert" on just about every phase of existence, says Harry Harris, TV critic of *The Philadelphia Inquirer.*

Hardly any TV program is duller than a static documentary. So a primary consideration is: is it interesting? Other factors:

Does the program cover the subject adequately in the allotted time? Should the program have been longer (or shorter)? Does it probe the question in depth or skim the surface? If the documentary deals with a controversial subject, does it shun the controversial aspects or plunge right in? Are both sides presented? Is the treatment convincing? Does the program make its points persuasively?

Persuasiveness is aided by the persons on the program. Acknowledged experts are an asset. So may be the man in the street if there is a suitable cross section.

Whether the program deals with ecology or drugs, is an examination of laws pertaining to guns, a star-conducted tour of a foreign capital, a survey of one of the arts, or a discussion of a human problem—does it leave the viewer satisfied? Or is something missing? Or is the program top-heavy in some respect? It is up to the receiver to assay the favorable and unfavorable points, the active credits, and the sins of omission as well as commission.

Many programs appeal to certain portions of the population—women or children, for instance. The reviewer may want to take a look at the debuts of specialized serials, and try to assess their quality and their effectiveness from the viewpoint of the desired audience. A further consideration is whether such a program will appeal to the population at large. Specialized programs of quality usually have wider appeal. The Columbia Broadcasting System's "Captain Kangaroo" and ABC's "Discovery," labeled children's programs, have a large percentage of adult viewers.

It is, of course, impossible for a man critic to review "As the World Turns" or "Sesame Street" from the viewpoint of a woman or child. He can present the at-large viewpoint. Here it may be helpful to have a wife or child, or handy facsimile, as a technical adviser.

The element of time sometimes creates problems. More than one attractive program, special or otherwise, may compete for attention with a show on another channel by overlapping all or in part. The at-home viewer must make a choice, or he can flip the dial. The critic must also make a choice, and watching two TV sets is hardly a solution. Like movie critics, he may have the opportunity to preview a program in a studio. A preview is especially helpful to a critic for a morning newspaper or a wire service who would otherwise have little time to write his review before deadline.

The time of presentation is sometimes open to criticism. A network may use poor judgment in scheduling a violent melodrama, or some other program unsuitable for children, at an early evening hour. Or it may present, late in the evening, a program that children would love and ought to see.

Too often a station will preempt a worthy network program for a locally sponsored offering of less quality or interest (but of greater financial return to the station). To nearly everyone, except the station officials, such preemptions seem to be made capriciously.

A station or network may present a worthwhile program at an hour inconvenient for much of its potential audience. But a trend toward repeats is evident. Acclaimed dramas or documentaries are almost certain to be rerun, sometimes within a few weeks or even a few days, often more than once. Public Broadcasting Service (formerly National Educational Television) and many independent stations schedule leading programs twice, as a matter of course. NBC added an immediate Sunday afternoon repeat of its Friday evening showing of *The Investigator,* Peter Weiss's controversial play.

Sometimes a documentary will spark national concern and even Congressional action. CBS' "Hunger in America," depicting the plight of migrant cropworkers, did that. A decade later an NBC documentary on the same subject, with the same producer, and using a few clips from the previous documentary, also provoked outraged comment and some hope of action.

TV critics are frustrated when meretricious programs continue because of good "ratings," and anthologies such as "ABC Stage 67" and "CBS Playhouse" go off the air despite critical accolades.

Yet TV critics do have influence, perhaps nowhere more effectively than when a consensus of bravos helps effect the rerun of an outstanding documentary or drama.

In recent years some networks and individual stations have shown previews and permitted, even encouraged, critics to print their reviews the day of the program rather than the day after. The idea is that, even if the review is unfavorable, calling attention to it in advance will make more people watch it.

Believe it or not, some televiewers object to this practice. They prefer to see the show themselves, without the critic's guideline, and to compare their own reactions with those of the critic the next day.

Of course, some televiewers are in the same category as some playgoers and music-lovers: They don't know what they think of the show until they read the review the next day. This remark is actually not as facetious as it seems. The review, as mentioned in an earlier chapter, clarifies things and, hopefully, makes its points in reasoned array. Most people do not expend the mental energy to do this; they wait for the review to do it for them.

* * *

Television drama is experiencing a new freedom, points out Harry Harris, television critic of *The Philadelphia Inquirer,* a freedom that had come earlier to the motion picture in America. Harris succinctly compares movies then and now. His qualitative comments on the TV drama reviewed are sprinkled through the article. He also gives a liberal sampling of quotations. (Technical note: He had probably received an advance copy of the script.)

> The TV times, they are a-changing. It used to be that the only way you could have a mateless hero or heroine with kids was to make him or her a widow or widower—and television series are still crammed with bereaved spouses.
>
> Divorce was a no-no. And as for TV's reflecting such modern mores as unmarried-and-proud-of-it motherhood, forget it!
>
> Now we have "Maude," with its title virago divorced THREE times! (And no wonder; how could any self-respecting male stay with her?) And telemovies are pointing the way to even more downloose (would that be the opposite of "uptight"?) programs.
>
> Take last night's ABC Movie of the Week, "Playmates."
>
> That was about a couple of divorced couples—affluent lawyer Alan ("M*A*S*H") Alda and neurotic, "artistic" Barbara Feldon; welder Doug ("Search") McClure and earthy, dance-happy Connie Stevens.
>
> The two papas, of unmarked dissimilar incomes and tastes, meet while squiring their young ones to an amusement park on visitation day.

They hit it off, get to meet each other's ex-wife while picking up the kids, and then remeet the girls on the sly.

Sex rears its ugly head, or whatever. Each member of the quadrangle is attracted by how the new lover differs from the old. For a while. Then the efforts of the better-educated partners to make their reluctant students more "culture"-minded begin to backfire.

When the welder discovers, through a remark by his son, that his lawyer buddy is "fooling around" with his former Mrs., violence erupts.

The welder returns to his satisfyingly simple-minded sexpot. The lawyer ALMOST manages a similar remarriage. The wry fadeout found him acquiring a new visitation-day buddy.

There were a number of unexpectedly "adult" twists in this bright, sprightly, well-acted comedy written by Richard Baer and directed by Theodore J. Flicker.

The two "seductions," for instance, were surprisingly forthright.

The lawyer, returning a forgotten beach bag, promptly made a pass at his buxom companion—and quickly apologized, "I never did anything so impetuous." To which she, smoldering, replied, "Did I complain?"

In the other romance, the Ms. took the initiative, announcing the first time they were alone, "I'd like you to take me."

"Take you where?"

"Here. Now."

"Why me?"

"You excite me, you rekindle basic urges. OK? . . . Morally, we're both adults, legally unattached."

"OK," he said, after a feeble "How about Marsh?", "You're the one who went to college."

Baer's script was studded with quips.

Of his former wife's love-making, for instance, the lawyer growled, "She never stopped talking. She was always coaching me. It was like being physical with Knute Rockne,"

And what kind of man would most appeal to an abstract-painting and health-food nut? "An avocado who owns an art gallery!"

In some ways this 90-minute milestone went beyond even yesteryear movie morality. In a Doris Day epic, for instance, the two couples would date, but not mate.

It still reflected a degree of caution, however, by limiting itself, at a time when there's much talk of wife-swapping, to considerably less shocking EX-wife-swapping.

* * *

The good old days of television and radio were good and not so good, reports Harry Harris in a twin review in *The Philadelphia Inquirer,* and so were the programs he considers. Again, succinct comments are interspersed with brief quotations.

Today's TV and yesteryear's radio were accorded 90-minute scrutinies last week.

Assorted critics eyed and decried video in ABC's "Wide World of Entertainment" entry, "TV Times," Thursday night. The tone was considerably more affectionate the following evening when five radio veterans, including Ezra Stone, for fifteen years Henry Aldrich in "The Aldrich Family," reminisced about the good old days on Channel 48's "Merv Griffin Show."

One thing "TV Times" demonstrated is that TV time is unlike any other kind.

"We'll be back in a moment," New York newsman Roger Grimsby, who co-hosted in thoroughly undistinguished manner with preening sportscaster Don Meredith, promised—or should that be warned?—at one point.

That "moment" managed to encompass commercials for feminine napkins, "A Touch of Grace," cold tablets and cook-in-bag foods.

The interruption would have been more irksome if what it interrupted had been more rewarding.

Rarely have so many "pundits" frittered away so much time to so little purpose.

The TV in "TV Times" could have stood for tedious vapidity. Not only were most of the comments inane, some were downright falsehoods.

For instance, conducting a poll of viewers, Meredith said, "Before this show is off the air, we may call you." How, when the program had been taped several nights earlier?

Harvey Orkin offered some amusing observations about soap operas and David Schoenbrun some astute ones about newscasts.

Otherwise, it was all not-so-clever carping by Kandy Stroud, whose assignment was gossip; Margot Hentoff, variety shows; Cleveland Amory, talkshows; George Lois, commercials, and Robert L. Greene, fashions.

* * *

There were more legitimate laughs in five minutes of Merv Griffin's convening of radio clowns Edgar Bergen, Hal (Throckmorton P. Gildersleeve) Peary, Ezra Stone and man-of-a-hundred-voices Mel Blanc plus "Lights Out" dramatist Arch Oboler, an unexpectedly funny guy himself, than in all of "TV Times."

Bergen told how his skill as a ventriloquist earned him a passing high school grade he didn't deserve and reminisced about his no-dummy dummy Charlie McCarthy. Did YOU know that a midget "played" Charlie in movies?

Peary and Blanc displayed their awesome vocal versatility—magical Mel, the voice of Barney Rubble in "The Flintstones," segued hilariously from Bugs Bunny to a wheezing Maxwell and a whinnying "English horse."

Stone, now primarily a TV and film director, recalled how an old actor's debt to his father was paid off in "elocution lessons" to correct a 7-year-old's lisp, and his subsequent show-biz debut on WCAU's "Children's Hour."

Oboler, in colorful jumpsuit ("I raise hippos"), reminded Bergen that he had scripted a controversial "Adam and Eve" skit for Charlie McCarthy and Mae West.

Obviously—and understandably—delighted by his guests' gab, Griffin indulged in some anecdotage, too—about his 1945 stint as a San Francisco station's "romantic mystery singer."

Although he was a Mutual network "star," fans were sent no pictures, he remembered wrly—and no wonder: he weighed 250 pounds and had a faceful of acne!

The only sample of an old broadcast was of Merv's long-ago warbling—sort of like inviting people over to look at home movies.

Oboler rated TV a lesser medium, because it requires no audience participation via imagination. "Radio," he opined, "was a pure art form."

Stone, bearded and balding—"Did you ever think you'd see Henry Aldrich in a beard?"—followed Griffin's fond farewells with an urgent request for help from his host: "Can you validate my parking ticket?"

Chapter XIII

REVIEW THE WORK AT HAND

Ideally, a reviewer should have read the book from which a play has been made; he should have seen the stage show from which the movie has been made. He should thus be able to make a natural comparison that many of his readers might also be able to make.

If he has not read the book or seen the show, he can still write an acceptable review of the thing he is seeing now. In fact, that is what he is supposed to do: review the current show.

His comparison of the previous and present media is merely to show how closely or not the show follows its ancestor. The amount of comparative detail depends on its importance, interest—and the space available for the review.

The important thing to remember is that you are reviewing the current show, not the book or play on which it is based. You can say, if possible, whether the movie is better than the stage show.

But primarily you review the show in terms of its own medium. *Dahlia's Dollhouse* was (or was not) a good play. Is it a good movie? Is the cinematic medium used to its optimum extent or does the movie seem to be merely a filmed stage play?

If it is a play or movie adapted to television, has the condensation to an hour (or 90 to 120 minutes, less commercials) been artistically accomplished, or are there gaps in the story and insufficiently developed characters?

If it is a book that has been dramatized, do the characters come to life? Does the whole story unfold on the stage or screen, or are there gaps? (If you have read the book, you can say which characters have been omitted. Does their omission tighten the story, or are these characters missed?)

The same factors are noted in a biography or other nonfiction made into a movie or play or TV show. It is of interest how well the change has been accomplished, but most of all, is it a good show?

If a show has been made from a biography, full-length or partial, does it hold interest? Does its drama stem from real-life sequence or from dramatic license? Are fictional characters introduced? Does the show concentrate unduly on too few persons or too few facets of the subject's career? Does it omit important facts? In other words, has the drama been transferred from life or has the writer felt it necessary to manufacture drama? In any case, is it a good play or movie? And are the impersonations valid?

In recent years there has been a trend toward reversing the former direction of stage play or musical to movie. Now some movies, and some TV plays, have been transformed into stage musicals. Lauren Bacall, once a movie star, became a stage star in *Applause,* a musical based on the movie *All About Eve.*

Of course there are many straight plays turned into musicals, on the stage and/or screen. *The Matchmaker* became *Hello, Dolly!, The Four-Poster* became *I Do! I Do!*

Bizet's opera *Carmen* was given a contemporary American setting as *Carmen Jones,* with different plot but with the music virtually intact. *The Mikado* became *The Hot Mikado,* a vehicle for the dancer Bill ("Bojangles") Robinson.

Many grand operas, especially in Europe, have been transferred to the movie screen. Note the use of the word "transferred," because in most cases that is exactly what the movie is, a filming of the opera from the opera-house stage. The opera is rarely filmed as a genuine motion picture, with added locales, because of the increased production costs and the feeling that audiences for screened grand operas are limited—and conservative: no "tampering" is allowed.

Sometimes imaginative use of the camera may bring adverse reaction. A movie of Moscow's famous Bolshoi Ballet in *The Sleeping Beauty* was criticized because of its special camera effects. Critics complained that the trick photography detracted from the overall effect; they said the dancing (aided by the music and scenic background) should have been allowed to speak for itself.

The critic may well be concerned with previous incarnations of the creative effort he is now reviewing, but his primary thought should be the use of the medium at hand.

Chapter XIV

MUSIC REVIEWING: T'NT AND THE SOLO ARTIST

Music is the most subjective and ephemeral of the arts. The same performance can move one listener to tears and make another gnash his teeth; it can keep some auditors on the edge of their seats and bore others. True, an audience is seldom split fifty-fifty with such reactions, but unless the performance is overpowering in its impact, or just plain terrible, there will probably be a majority and minority who are affected positively or negatively at every concert hall.

Listening to music is compounded of many factors. The recitalist may be an idol, and can do no wrong—even when he or she does. The program may be a surefire audience-pleaser, or may be entirely made up of new music that can wear out the audience—and the critics. The critic may be overly tired, or didn't enjoy his dinner, or had a quarrel with his wife. Or there may be other reasons that make it hard to concentrate on the music.

In any event, in music, as on any other occasion when he is "working," the critic does not sit back in his chair. Paying members of the audience may relax; they may even fall asleep (that is one form of criticism!). The reviewer must be alert for as many details of the performance as he can encompass. Although he is not relaxed, this is more than compensated for because he will get more out of the performance.

Concerts, as well as stage plays, are ephemeral in that they affect only those who hear that performance. Minutes later they are gone forever (unless taped for broadcast or recordings). But a memorable performance will never be absent from the mind of a perspicacious, appreciative listener. Certain details of a concert or opera will live in one's mind long after the rest of the concert is forgotten. One example is a final soft note beautifully sustained by Richard Tauber, the great German tenor. It came at the end of his recital, and some in the audience may have missed it; those who heard it probably still remember it.

Others appreciatively recall having heard, perhaps frequently, an exciting concerto performance by Van Cliburn, an illuminative interpretation of Chopin by Artur Rubinstein, a volatile Wagner excerpt or orchestral transcription of Bach by Leopold Stokowski, a tonally rich Brahms symphony by the Philadelphia Orchestra under Eugene Ormandy, a precise musical evocation by Arturo Toscanini or George Szell, a stratospheric operatic performance by Joan Sutherland or Beverly Sills.

Critics seldom leave their jobs except by death or retirement. They are in love with their art form—music, the theater, motion pictures, television, the dance, literature, the fine arts. Every event they review has an air of adventure about it. They are always hoping for something worthwhile—a recommendable new play or movie, a great performance, a new author, musical artist, painter, or sculptor with something to say.

Great plays bear repeating, and great musical works are heard constantly. There is room for variety in performances of Hamlet, Annie Oakley, Carmen, and Beethoven symphonies, in biographies of George Washington, and in interpretations of a landscape or a nude from realistic to futuristic.

This brief interpolation may offer one explanation of the magic of the performing arts to both layman and critic. Now we deal with the most magical art of all, the one that William Congreve said "hath charms to soothe the savage breast, to soften rocks, or bend a knotted oak."

What's T'NT? It comprises the three principal factors of any solo recital, and the order of their importance will vary: Tone, 'Nterpretation, and Technique. Ordinarily interpretation takes precedence; indeed, like the baseball pitcher who no longer has a fast ball but gets by on sheer cunning and control, an artist past his or her tonal or technical prime may still enchant audiences through winning interpretation.

Here again, the subjectiveness of musical listening is emphasized. One critic will be moved by an interpretation despite deficiency in technique; another critic may say that technical deficiency ruined the interpretation.

First the tone. Is the sound you hear from the solo singer or instrumentalist resonant, rich, full, sonorous, bright, dull, dry, brittle, pinched? Is it varied as to dynamics (gradations of volume) and coloring? Does the recitalist have control of his tone? Are the sounds he produces those he apparently wants?

Is the singer's voice even in its various "registers"? Is it more, or less, powerful at the top or bottom or in the middle? And are there holes in the compass? Is the singer's range adequate for the music he is performing, or are there danger spots at the top and bottom?

Keyboard recitalists excepted, does the recitalist perform on pitch —in other words, how is his intonation? A vocalist may consistently sing flat or sharp, a string or wind instrumentalist may play that way. Occasionally a contemporary composer may call for quarter tones, but in that case the player may explain this to the audience beforehand.

Does the instrumentalist manage his tone nicely? Does the pianist's left hand overshadow his right? Is the keyboard, string, or wind tone balanced and freely produced?

Is the recitalist's technique sufficient for the music being performed? Does the recitalist use technique (and tone) in the service of interpretation, or as an end in itself? If an instrumentalist plays something as fast as possible, using virtuosity for its own sake, or if a singer bellows where some vocal finesse is called for, this practice should be condemned. On the other hand, he may play or sing something so slowly as to drain it of life.

Does the singer or player perform scale and other rapid passages smoothly? Does the singer use, or overuse, portamento (tying notes of wide intervals)? Does the singer or wind player have good breath control, ease of phrasing? Can the singer, pianist, or other instrumentalist manage evenness of repeated notes, or a graduated crescendo or decrescendo, when called for? (Control of dynamics, again.)

Is the recitalist's thundering or whispering appropriate to the music? Operatic arias and songs are not necessarily shouted. Scarlatti sonatas do not demand excess speed; they do demand good tonal control.

Does the soloist tailor his tone to the music at hand? A Fauré song is not performed like a Wagner aria. A Mozart sonata shouldn't sound like late Beethoven.

How are the pianist's arpeggios and chord passages? Does the violinist or cellist handle his bow well, or is his bow-arm technique unwieldy? Is his fingering rapid, smooth, or slovenly? Are his double stops (playing two notes at a time) and harmonics ('way up in the scale) accurate?

A pipe organist, like any other recitalist, is limited by the instrument on which he performs. He cannot vary the tonal volume by touch, but only by mechanical means—the swell or expression pedal, and by adding or subtracting stops.

How well does the organist use the resources of the instrument? Does his registration (choice of stops) seem appropriate to the music? There are four families of organ tone: diapason (fundamental organ tone), reeds, flutes, and strings; does the organist use them in a musical manner, or is there an overabundance of reeds and mixtures? Or is his coloring bland or monotonous?

Is the organist's manual (keyboard) and pedal (playing the notes with his feet) technique smooth and speedy? How is his legato touch —smooth?

We have touched on interpretation in the preceding pages. But one always returns to interpretation. Satisfactory interpretation is the *raison d'être* of any piece on the program. The recitalist's technique should be equal to any interpretive demands of the artist or the music.

Does the recitalist get to the heart of the music or merely skim the surface? (This, of course, applies to the performance of any musical composition. On other occasions, this appraisal is made of the conductor.) Does he convey the mood of the work convincingly? A vocal or instrumental number performed in the wrong style can be grotesque. Does the performer have a command of the various styles required in the program? If, by mischance, everything is in the same style, does the artist nevertheless maintain interest throughout the evening?

In a word, does the artist communicate?

Does the instrumentalist delineate effectively the architecture of a sonata or other major composition? Is his playing of a theme and variations clear or turgid? Is there more than mere technique to his playing of a brilliant, technically demanding work? Even the Tchaikovsky *First Piano Concerto* can be a piece of music, but it takes a superior artist, such as Gilels or Rubinstein, to play it with more than technique and to convey its musical values. The same can apply to some pyrotechnical Liszt piano works or Paganini violin pieces.

Is the recitalist's performance of a piece of music finely detailed or overly fussy? A recitalist can be enthralled by the trees and be unaware of the forest. A critic can also be preoccupied with details and miss the larger picture.

As in his review of a show, the critic should strive to convey the principal effect of the musical program, using details to buttress his major premise. He need not discuss the music in the order of its performance, nor need he mention every number on the program.

Also, as with a show, the critic may find exceptions to his major premise, but the exceptions should not outweigh the general verdict, lest the reviewer contradict himself. One may praise a recitalist's tone and technique, yet call his interpretations shallow. Also, a performer may lack the ultimate in tone or technique, but still be a compelling artist.

The accompanist, although not paid nearly as much as the recital star, is an important part of the program. A good accompanist can enhance a recital, a poor one can mar or ruin it.

Some concert pianists turn with ease to accompanying or chamber music. Others have forgone solo careers and won fame as accompanists—Gerald Moore is the outstanding example. The names of some pianists are coupled with their soloists—Fritz Kreisler and Carl Lamson, Marian Anderson and Franz Rupp, David Oistrakh and Vladimir Yampolsky.

The pianist must be sympathetic (not in the sense of feeling sorry for) with the soloist. He should be thoroughly in accord with the soloist's interpretations and follow them, maintaining the proper tempo and complementing, but not drowning out, the violinist or singer (one may occasionally wish he would!). Nor should he be so self-effacing that the accompaniment lacks body.

Note that in a violin, 'cello, clarinet, or flute *sonata,* the piano is equal with the other instrument. The pianist is a collaborator here, not an accompanist. In some passages he may properly all but drown out the string or wind instrument.

In piano duets (four hands at one keyboard) or in duo-piano recitals (two pianos), the ensemble and rapport between the pianists is the key to the quality of the recital. Neither pianist should overshadow the other, but this happens all too often, especially in husband-and-wife amateur piano duos. Sometimes the duet player of the upper half (primo) and lower half (secondo) will exchange positions, or the duo-pianists will switch instruments, to give visual variety and to show that they can maintain tonal balance either way.

In four-hand piano recitals, the music should speak as if from one player. Unity of ensemble, or agreement (rapport) in details of interpretation, is the principal factor.

* * *

Harold C. Schonberg, music critic of *The New York Times,* appraises the artistry of the famous German baritone Dietrich Fischer-Dieskau from a broad viewpoint of the artist's long and distinguished career.

Dietrich Fischer-Dieskau, who has the biggest repertory of any singer who ever lived, who has made more recordings than anybody else in history, who continues to look younger as the years go on, returned to Carnegie Hall on Tuesday evening. With Guenther Weissenborn at the piano, the celebrated baritone sang a program devoted exclusively to the songs of Brahms.

He picked the songs very carefully, for the most part avoiding the better-known ones, trying to cover the expressive gamut of the Brahms lieder. The evening was one of contrasts, with a rhapsodic song such as "Auf dem See" juxtaposed to the hushed lyricism of "Nachtwandler," which in turn was offset by the dramatic sweep of "Wehe, so willst du mich wieder." As song succeeded song, one could revel in the luxurious variety of the material—and also realize that the Brahms songs contain masterpiece after masterpiece.

Mr. Fischer-Dieskau's singing pursued its familiar course. As always with him, it was not so much a question of voice qua voice as it was the way the voice was used. And that of course is where the baritone's supreme artistry enters. He is a master at the long legato line, and at the ability to space out a song, stressing exactly the things that need stressing.

Above all there is his uncanny ability to supply verbal as well as musical coloration. This is not only a matter of clear diction. Mr. Fischer-Dieskau seizes upon certain words in a song and, with subtle inflection and emphases, brings out the music of the poetry itself.

Thus one can ignore a few vocal deficiencies in the singer's equipment —an occasional forced high note, or a series of less than sensuous sounds. In any case, these did not often happen. Mr. Fischer-Dieskau is too brainy a singer to select material that caters to his technical weaknesses.

And so, for the most part, what Mr. Fischer-Dieskau sang, he sang perfectly. He brought a prevailingly quiet, intimate vocal quality to the music, but within this framework there were all kinds of dynamic inflections. Fortissimos were sparsely used, and when they were, they sounded thunderous and that much more meaningful. Mr. Fischer-Dieskau as a recitalist woos rather than assaults.

There was no one song that could be picked out. Everything was on the highest level of artistry, and the essence of every song was captured. Long past are the days when Mr. Fischer-Dieskau could be arch in the lighter songs. Now, as in the "Staendchen" of Opus 106, he captures a light mood without being obvious about it. And when it comes to the nobility of such a song as "Wie bist du, meine Koenigen," or the intensity of "Botschaft," or the yearning quality of "Fruehlingslied," Mr. Fischer-Dieskau is the complete interpreter, singing with maturity, style, and infinite resource.

As many additional listeners as could be accommodated on the stage of Carnegie Hall supplemented the regular audience. Mr. Weissenborn supplied solid backgrounds at the piano and was rewarded at the end by a hug from the big baritone. (Copyright *The New York Times*).

* * *

The phenomenal Artur Rubinstein is given an appraisal as fresh as his playing, in this review by Samuel L. Singer of *The Philadelphia Inquirer*. The review appeared twelve days before Rubinstein's 87th birthday on January 28, 1973. (The pianist probably gave a recital that day to celebrate.)

Get out that lead we use for every Artur Rubinstein recital: The season's largest Academy of Music audience heard the octogenarian pianist Monday evening.

The reason is simple: Except for Van Cliburn, Rubinstein is the only artist who not only can sell stage seats but allows them. There were about 150 seated on stage, and the piano was moved to right center so that more than half the audience could watch those fabulous fingers.

This wunderkind, who will be a mere 87 years old a week from next Sunday, never fails to offer a mixture of surprise and delight on his programs.

While his stage demeanor and musicianship are as dependable as ever, he dares to be different in his playing.

Music Reviewing: T'NT and the Solo Artist

The approach has for decades been one of mellow maturity. Yet the surprise and delight are supplied by a just-as-dependable element of freshness.

Pianists half or a quarter Rubinstein's age start the Bach-Busoni Chaconne (from the Violin Partita No. 2) with magisterial chords and go on from there. Rubinstein played the opening comparatively softly, allowing greater variety in his tonal palette and enabling him to build to the climax convincingly without pounding.

The understatement was effective throughout the recital. There was

Pianist Artur Rubenstein remains an unexcelled artist and a leading concert attraction even in his 80's.

subdued power in "Aufschwung," the second of Schumann's eight Fantasy Pieces, and a gentle fire in "In der Nacht." "Warum?", the best-known piece of the set, was a whispered, plaintive question. "Traumes-wirren" enjoyed a marvelous lightness of touch that was feathery but clear. The whole cycle breathed the poetry of the Romantic.

So did Chopin's Sonata No. 3 in B minor, played with a singing tone from beginning to end. One concentrated here not on technique, although Rubinstein demonstrated ample dexterity in the two fast movements, but on the many glints and sidelights which make every Rubinstein interpretation of Chopin an event.

There was discreet use of rubato, just the proper soupçon, in the opening movement, while the Largo was marked by a smooth, easy flow that made it a treasurable song.

Unlike most pianists, all of whom are younger than he, Rubinstein plays with hardly any movement other than of his hands and fingers, permitting exclusive attention to the music, nor does he take a break between major sections of the program.

Thus he played 40 or 45 minutes at a time, the Chopin Sonata following the Chaconne, and Liszt's "Valse Oubliée" and Hungarian Rhapsody No. 12 following the Schumann.

Even at nearly 87, Rubinstein can do no wrong and, as many times before, one forgives some missed notes and an occasional muddiness (as in the Chaconne). But the little man who is much bigger than his size refuses to occupy any pedestal.

Rubinstein is accustomed to standing ovations. This audience gave him one, and would have liked more than the three encores this ageless artist gave them: Chabrier's Scherzo-Valse, Mendelssohn's "Spinning Song," and the Villa-Lobos "Punchinello."

Chapter XV

INSTRUMENTAL AND VOCAL ENSEMBLES— AND CONDUCTORS

Most of the qualities that you seek in a solo recital also are to be listened for in a concert by an orchestra, chorus, quartet, or other ensemble. One difference is that the pitfalls are multiplied, figuratively, by the number of performers—one faulty player or singer can damage a piece of music or even the whole concert.

Usually the center of attraction is the conductor—he gets the credit and the blame. He is praised for an inspired performance, castigated for a pedestrian one. He usually deserves what he gets.

The performers, of course, must cooperate. A college or professional team may play above its theoretical capacity for an inspiring coach or manager. A coach or manager who uses poor psychology, or is technically incompetent, will not get the maximum results from his players.

The same may be said for conductors. A great symphony or choral director may inspire an orchestra to play above its head, or a chorus to sing its heart out. And a dull conductor will elicit dull response, even from a highly professional ensemble.

Here, as in solo recitals, music is subjective. Great music greatly performed will send the audience—and even the critics—home walking on air. (I was tempted to omit the last four words. A great performance should "send" you.) And a great performance is a team proposition—perfect rapport between conductor and ensemble.

Since a conductor is responsible for the performance, he should obtain the results he wants. The orchestra or chorus should be responsive and flexible. If the conductor seeks broad effects or delicacy of nuance, he should obtain them through his podium skill and the alertness of his musicians. If the conductor does not have enough podium technique, the necessary ability to use his arms and hands to make his wants known, he should not be there.

The conductor's movements are necessary, but ideally they should be as unobtrusive as possible; that is, they should not prove a distraction to the audience (or the performers). Some concert pianists (Glenn Gould, sometimes Rudolf Serkin) gyrate about the keyboard so much that one must close one's eyes to hear the music. Some singers make such faces when singing that you are liable to forget the sound. And while a conductor may often wave his arms forcefully, and sometimes move his head, he need not do a podium dance or calisthenics. Such outsized movements may have no bearing on the sound of the music, although the conductor thinks they do, but they can influence the listener's enjoyment.

The podium deportment of a new conductor or a guest is worthy of mention, even if it is merely described without praise or derogation. The conductor is the star of the show, and the way he looks and acts, in addition to the results he obtains, is a matter of interest.

The question of new music has been considered earlier. A listener's firmest basis for appraising the qualities of a conductor is in hearing a standard work. European and American orchestras have different sounds: one is lean, the other lush. European and American conductors have different ideas. By and large, U.S. conductors take music at a faster tempo than their Continental confreres.

A European conductor, interpreting a Beethoven symphony at a slower pace than the audience is used to, may be accused of dullness and lethargy, or he may be praised for the breadth, the serenity, the enriching detail, the soft glow that he brings to the music.

Just as the qualities of a symphonic or choral conductor are much the same, so with the ensemble. Is it well balanced? Are the "choirs" of the orchestra—the strings, woodwinds, and brass (and percussion)—individually and collectively worthy? Do the sections of the chorus—sopranos, altos, tenors, and basses—balance, in tone if not in numbers? The usual amateur chorus has at least twice as many women singers as men, yet somehow the men manage to make themselves heard (the lower voices are heavier), and often the tonal balance is surprisingly good.

Tonal criteria for the ensemble are much the same as for the solo artist: resonant, rich, full, sonorous, bright, dull, dry, brittle, pinched? Is it truly an ensemble tone, or do you hear individual players or voices when you shouldn't? (One exceptional voice should never stand out in a chorus unless in a solo passage.) The intonation of a professional orchestra seldom will be at fault, but do the chorus members sing on pitch? Particularly in an unaccompanied number, is the intonation steady?

If the playing or singing is taut and responsive, if the conductor seems to be getting just the results he wants, the podium artist is to be praised—for his command of the ensemble, if not for his interpretations. If the performance is slipshod, the ensemble ragged, the conductor is a faulty disciplinarian. Uninspired singing or playing generally is the reward of an uninspiring conductor.

Aside from expression in the music, an ensemble may be judged in one elementary way—its attacks and releases. In other words, do the players or singers all enter together and finish together? Shoddy ensemble in this respect is chargeable to the conductor.

Again, as in the solo recital, does the performer—in this case, the conductor—get to the heart of the music? Does he interpret each piece in its proper style? Does he use the ability of his ensemble in the service of the music, or does he sometimes seek virtuoso effects for their own sake? Some choral directors—one remembers the diminutive Serge Jaroff of the Don Cossacks Choir in this respect—love to perform sudden, shattering diminuendos and crescendos, often for no apparent reason. This is akin to the piano-pounder and the bellowing tenor or shrieking soprano who use volume or other technical display, just for display.

The conductor of a fine orchestra is fortunate to have such an instrument at his disposal. Most often, he deserves credit for having built such an ensemble. But he must use it musically, not misuse it.

The question of style is often raised. Should Mozart and Haydn symphonies always be played by an orchestra the size of that in the composer's day? Is it artistic when played by virtually the full ensemble? How do Bach's choral masterworks appeal to you when sung by a massive chorus several times larger than Bach's eighteenth-century choir? Some conductors use different-sized choruses for various passages in such works as Handel's *Messiah,* to achieve clarity in the vocal lines as contrasted with sonority. How does this practice affect the effect?

Conductors usually reply to criticism of style by saying, "The composer didn't dream of the marvelous twentieth-century symphony orchestra." Or, "I find things in the music the composer didn't know were there." Some conductors, carried away by the rich sound of their ensembles, try to make Mozart sound like Brahms.

The critic, when assaying these practices, is either too lenient or

Eugene Ormandy, one of the top box-office draws among symphony conductors, has led the Philadelphia Orchestra since 1936. This is a record unmatched by any head of a major symphony orchestra. Ormandy is only the fourth musical director of the Philadelphia Orchestra, which was founded in 1900 and achieved world fame under Leopold Stokowski, its conductor for nearly thirty years.

too narrow-minded, depending on the views of the tradition-minded or broad-minded reader or listener.

When there is a soloist, the ensemble is an accompanying instrument. The conductor leads the orchestra and should see to it that the orchestra (or chorus) does not drown out the solo performer. Moreover, he should pace the orchestra according to the soloist's tempo. Differences of opinion as to interpretation, including tempo, should be worked out in rehearsal. Several times in recent years conductors and virtuosos have disagreed publicly on fundamental interpretation. In one case, the soloist walked out; in another, the conductor disclaimed, to the audience, any responsibility for the way the concerto was about to be performed. It is rare when such differences in views on interpretation are irreconcilable. When they are, the audience is usually the loser. A reviewer should be able to spot when a conductor and soloist are straining at their leashes.

Overall, the concerto should have unity of ensemble in performance and interpretation. Soloist, conductor, and orchestra should be of one musical mind. The accompaniment should be well balanced, neither diffident nor overpowering; it should complement the soloist.

The quartet, quintet, or other chamber ensemble almost always performs without a conductor. Here the credit or discredit is bestowed collectively, not on an individual.

And how did our little quartet play tonight? Tonal and ensemble criteria are applied in toto. If one instrument (or one voice) stands out too often, the ensemble is faulty.

Intonation is usually measured by the group, but a violinist or singer off pitch may be spotted. The technique of the performers individually and collectively should be equal to the music at hand.

With chamber ensembles, since there is no conductor, the members at rehearsal should agree on details of interpretation. Is the rapport good? Does the music seem to come from one instrument instead of four or five? Does the music, sometimes a theme or other melodic line, flow freely from one instrument (or singer) to another? Is a set of variations, as in a Schubert or Beethoven quartet, clearly delineated?

Is the ensemble balanced? Do the various instruments give a satisfying total effect despite their individuality? Do the instruments blend well, yet retain their desirable differing tonal characteristics?

The question of balance is notable in a piano trio or quartet, in which the keyboard instrumentalist must be careful not to overpower his two or three string-playing colleagues. Sometimes, as in a Brahms quartet, which may be "a piano solo with string trio," the pianist may be hard put to keep himself in check. The string players generally should not have to force their tone to be heard.

Here is the story that was cited in Chapter III.

The review was shorter than it ordinarily would have been, because a two-column picture was used in the adjoining space.

The article was written to fit an awkward space above advertisements, across four columns. Note that the last paragraph can be omitted, and the last sentence may be cut, phrase by phrase.

Pianists at Academy

Mutt Butts In on Masters' Bach

By Samuel L. Singer

A silent partner in the musical firm of Luboshutz and Nemenoff, duo-pianists, all but stole the show with a brief and definitely unscheduled appearance on the Academy of Music stage last night.

The scene-stealer was Vodka, combination setter and cocker spaniel of the Luboshutzes (Miss Nemenoff is Mrs. L. in private life), who walked out on the stage during the playing of Bach's Three-Piano Concerto in C. Vodka calmly surveyed the scene, then settled quietly at Miss Nemenoff's feet for the rest of the concerto. Nobody, including Luboshutz's nephew, Boris Goldovsky, who was conducting from the third piano, missed a beat.

At a concert of less musical stature, Vodka's presence might have proved disturbing. But such artists as these three star pianists took the dog's presence in stride, and so did the audience.

"Vodka sits for hours under the piano at home," Miss Nemenoff said at intermission. "I never should have brought him from the hotel, but he was so lonely there. And I thought the dressing-room door was closed."

This concert, which closed the Philadelphia All Star Concert Series (a division of The Philadelphia Inquirer Charities), was an outgrowth of the pianist trio's highly successful Mozart program of two seasons ago. This time, as then, Goldovsky conducted, except when he was soloist in a one-piano concerto, when Uncle Pierre directed.

The program opened with Weber's "Peter Schmoll" Overture. The aforementioned Bach Concerto was played with superb evenness in dynamic gradations, gentle waves of sound ebbing and flowing. The strings sang in the slow movement of the Shostakovich Concerto for Piano, Trumpet and Strings, with Goldovsky at the keyboard.

Martinu's Two-Piano Concerto found L & N at their best. It is a work of shifting moods, energetic, rather goodnatured in the fast outer movements; generally contemplative, with mild dissonance, in the slow movement.

The program ended with Luboshutz' expert Fantasy on Themes from Strauss's "Fledermaus," with three pianos and orchestra.

Emma Feldman, director of the concert series since its inception in 1934, was given a framed citation from Mayor Richardson Dilworth in anticipation of her 25th season. The surprise award was affectionately presented by Mrs. Fredric R. Mann, wife of the City Representative, who justly termed Miss Feldman "Miss Impresario" of Philadelphia.

* * *

An earlier performance by Luboshutz and Nemenoff, with the Philadelphia Orchestra, is presented.

The article illustrates the compulsive alliteration for which the late Linton Martin, longtime music editor of *The Philadelphia Inquirer,* was famous.

Mozart 2-Piano Concerto Is Featured by Orchestra

By Linton Martin

PROGRAM
Handel .. "Messiah": Pastoral Symphony
Mozart
    Two-Piano Concerto in E-flat major
Wagner .... "Tannhaeuser" Overture
"A Siegfried Idyll"
"Meistersinger" Excerpts"

A pair of peerless piano soloists, for the usual price of one, was the opulently artistic offering which Eugene Ormandy, as something of a symphonic Santa, presented on his Yuletide program at the Philadelphia Orchestra concert in the Academy yesterday. He also included a couple of numbers specifically inspired by the Christmas season and intended for its celebration.

The gifted pianistic partners were Pierre Luboshutz and Genia Nemenoff, whose superb performance of Mozart's Two-Piano Concerto in E-flat major marked their first appearance as symphony soloists here in four seasons. The Christmas season salutations were the exquisite orchestral interlude of the Pastoral Symphony from Handel's "Messiah," and Wagner's "A Siegfried Idyll," with the rest of the program devoted to other Wagnerian numbers: the "Tannhaeuser" Overture, and several "Meistersinger" excerpts consisting of the Third Act Prelude, Dance of the Apprentices, and the Entrance of the Masters.

A quite captivating display of triumphant teamwork, in tone and technique, was vouchsafed the enchanted symphony subscribers in the playing of the Mozart concerto by Luboshutz and Miss Nemenoff. Perhaps such professional compatibility was simply to be expected of pianistic partners who, as husband and wife, are also personal partners in private life. But such complete accord in sensitive understanding and artistry of expression is exceptional.

Indeed, in certain closely interrelated piano passages, the ear required the aid of the eye, in identifying the personal participation of the soloists. For theirs is the art of duo-pianism at its peak of perfection, and which goes far beyond the externals of interpretive eloquence of expression.

Keeping clearly in mind the classic character and content of the concerto, their performance was marked by admirably adjusted delicacy of dynamic detail, but with not the slightest sacrifice of vitality or vigor. For they manage remarkably to achieve refinement that is never effete, but rewardingly robust, and in sheer beauty of poetic persuasiveness, their playing of this Mozart work was more revealing of their resources than the larger concert canvas of the modern Martinu concerto for two pianos that they introduced here four years ago.

Ormandy and the orchestra gave the soloists the finest possible support, in that the pianistic performance was never shouldered or overshadowed, thus meticulously observing Mozart's intentions in his instrumentation.

The opening excerpt from the Handel oratorio suitably set the musical mood for the season, and the Wagnerian works after the intermission were played with communicative enthusiasm.

Chapter XVI

GRAND OPERA

Opera is drama, sometimes comedy, that is sung instead of spoken, and has orchestral accompaniment. There may or may not be ballet. There is generally a chorus, but not all grand operas use one. Whereas in musical comedy the singing and dancing choruses are often the same, in opera the ballet dancers rarely sing, the chorus rarely dances. (Sometimes the ballet can't dance and the chorus can't sing, but that's something else again.)

Although the same criteria apply to operas as to musical stage productions, the emphasis, especially with grand opera, is on the musical factors and not on the story or decor. Verdi's *Il Trovatore,* a prime example of incredible, mixed-up plot, survives because of its abundance of good tunes. With most operas in the standard repertory, there is a dramatic, viable libretto as well as good music. Often, as in the case of Weber's operas, good music has not been enough to offset an inept libretto.

Exotic settings and wonderful music are not the only things that have placed *La Bohème, Madame Butterfly, Carmen, La Traviata,* and *Aida*—to name but five—among the most popular grand operas. The characters are able to stir the members of the audience, who sympathize with their predicaments. Often it is not just sympathy but empathy.

These operas are not cited as the five greatest. Others—by Wagner, Mozart, or Verdi—may have higher stature but are given less frequently because they cost more to produce; they need more first-line singers, more opulent staging, and perhaps a larger orchestra.

A goodly proportion of all operas to be reviewed are from the five named. Assuming you are covering an opera from the staple repertoire, your checklist of items is a combination of those from the theater and concert platforms. The order of importance depends on the performance, but in grand opera the singing usually receives first attention.

The central character of an opera such as *Carmen* or *La Traviata* can make or break a performance. The surrounding singers, decor, and orchestral accompaniment must be pretty effective to offset a schoolmarmish Carmen. On the other hand, a vital Carmen with a sensuous voice can (but does not always) overcome an otherwise shoddy production.

Great opera singers can and do get away with murder as to visual effectiveness. A former rule of thumb for the singer of the title role in *Carmen* was that she should not weigh more than the bull. Within this writer's career as a music critic not only have Carmens slimmed down, but the standard of stage verisimilitude has risen perceptibly. (This is in line with raised standards of instrumental performance, too. Technique of soloists and ensembles is taken for granted. It was not always thus.)

Depending on the length of the opera and the role, an artist may sing more in one opera than in an entire recital, yet a recital may be more difficult—for some artists—because of its musical diversity: many composers, many styles.

The qualities of the voice and the interpretation in opera necessarily differ from a recital, since they are centered on one character instead of many protagonists. The technical factors are all there, although differing in degree of application: tonal quality and volume, finesse in detail, diction, phrasing. The opera star sings more in full voice—and her gestures are broader—because the opera house is usually larger than the recital hall. But the great artist's performance does not lack nicety of detail, vocal and visual.

Because the voice is the prime requisite, the opera stars often do little else than sing when on stage. Admittedly it is harder to be a great actor when you have to sing instead of talk. But it can be done. Chaliapin is remembered as much for his ability as an actor, whether in *Boris Godunov* or *The Barber of Seville,* as for his unsurpassed basso voice. Today, however, the emergence (or reascendance) of the opera stage director's power has resulted in dramatic performances that complement the fine singing. (These remarks rarely apply to tenors, especially Italian tenors. A star tenor is a law unto himself; any credible acting beyond the bare essentials may be considered a bonus.)

The example of a fast-ball pitcher whose cunning increases as his speed declines, thereby keeping him in the major leagues, was cited previously. The illustration may again serve, regarding opera singers. A bellowing tenor, a soprano with gorgeous top tones, may achieve stardom on the basis of sheer vocal power. If there is any brain behind that voice machine, the stage deportment will improve, the interpretation will mellow and deepen. There may come a time when maturity of dramatic interpretation will outweigh the vocal factors.

The critic will readily observe, too, that the soprano is rarely as young as the stage heroine she is portraying. And does the tenor's fine singing of the hero overcome the tenor's age? An opera singer's prime is roughly the years from 30 to 50. Some reach stardom in their 20's; others continue as prime attractions into their upper 50's. The durable Jan Peerce, whose vocal career has spanned four decades, sang the Duke in *Rigoletto* with the Philadelphia Grand Opera Company when over the age of 60, and his singing and acting had the freshness of youth.

In a recital, the critic assays the soloist's ability to communicate the moods of various arias and songs. In an opera, the singer may run the gamut of emotions in portraying a single character. Aida is torn between love for Radames and love of her conquered country. Rigoletto loves his daughter, Gilda, and hates and despises the profligate Duke whom he serves as jester and the Duke's fawning courtiers. Love and hate in the same woman, perhaps for the same man, occur frequently in operas from *Norma* to *Elektra*. Romantic love and jealousy are combined in a masterful quartet in the third act of *La Bohème*. How about those love potions, real or imagined, in operas ranging from *Tristan and Isolde* to *The Elixir of Love?* The composer has written instant emotional changes in the music, but the singers and orchestra must convey them.

It is up to the reviewer to judge whether the opera star's performance is well rounded. How effective is it, and why? Does the quality of the singing (good or bad!) make one forget the acting, or vice versa? Are the singing and acting of equal or nearly equal merit? Are they consistent in quality? Often it takes an opera star an act or two to warm up, and the portrayal in the last act will be noticeably better than in the first act. "Celeste Aida," the tenor's big aria in *Aida,* is always regarded as a particular hardship for the singer because it occurs so near the beginning of the opera.

98   The Student Journalist and Reviewing the Performing Arts

Singing of key arias and other numbers—famous duets, trios, quartets—is mentioned, as a rule, when describing a performance. In some operas the audience lives for just one aria, and hardly anything else matters. "One fine day" in *Madame Butterfly* is an illustration. You can review the performance, and describe Butterfly's acting and singing in vivid detail, yet if you fail to mention how she sang

The Mad Scene from *Lucia di Lammermoor* is one of the great musical and dramatic opportunities for the coloratura soprano. Here is Beverly Sills in the title role of the Donizetti masterpiece, just after Lucia has stabbed her bridegroom.

"Un bel dì"—it probably stopped the show—your readers will feel cheated. Ditto for "Una furtiva lagrima" in *L'Elisir d'Amore*.

Similar examples abound in other operas. Carmen herself has numerous vocal opportunities, but what about the tenor's Flower Song, the baritone's Toreador Song, and Micaela's one or two arias? You can hardly avoid mentioning "Vissi d'arte" in *Tosca,* "Caro nome" and the Quartet in *Rigoletto,* the Mad Scene (and the Sextet) in *Lucia di Lammermoor,* the Jewel Song in *Faust,* "Sempre libera" and "Ah! fors' è lui" in *La Traviata,* "Ritorna vincitor" in *Aida,* "In questi reggia" in *Turandot.* The list is endless. Not only are they famous numbers often heard in concert or on records, but they describe musically the nature of the character being portrayed.

The performance of the lead is, of course, only one factor, albeit generally the major factor, of the production.

Sit back and take an overall look (and listen) at the opera. How is it, everything considered? Regardless of the individual merit of the stars, do they fit into the ensemble or are they virtually on their own? Does the conductor have the singers and orchestra in hand? Do the conductor and the stars and the chorus have the same idea about such things as tempo? Are the stars (just as in a stage play) sure of their lines or do they need undue help from the prompters or are their eyes glued to the conductor's baton? Does the conductor keep the orchestra in proper proportion or does he sometimes (perhaps mercifully) drown out the singers? Is the orchestra playing well or is it underrehearsed?

The stage director has recently assumed, or resumed, importance in the operatic scheme of things. For good or ill, is the presence of the stage director felt? Do his instructions to the principals and chorus make sense? Or do the singers give the impression of no direction, or lackadaisical direction? Is the stage direction in keeping with the style of the opera?

Has the opera been staged according to its original setting, or has the place or period been changed? Verdi's *Masked Ball,* based on a Swedish king's assassination, was transferred to a Colonial Boston setting, complete with a "Count of Boston," to appease the censors. Nowadays its true setting and time period are often used. (*Hamlet* and other Shakespearean plays have been given in modern dress.) If a change has been made, is it dramatically effective?

In any event, as with spoken plays, do the settings and costumes aid the production? Are they sumptuous, frugal, or in between? Are they realistic or stylized? Do they reflect creativity and good taste? If the opera is given by a repertory company, sometimes economy is practiced in the use of shabby, worn sets or a setting from some other opera.

Are the costumes appropriate? Are there slipshod details, such as the nuns in *Sister Angelica* wearing high heels and perhaps wristwatches? Does a star's ill-fitting, ill-colored wig annoy your eye?

How good is the ballet contribution, if any? Does it enhance or merely interrupt the performance? Appraise the leading dancers, the corps de ballet, and the choreography.

All the foregoing comments, while primarily concerned with appraisal of familiar operas, apply to new operas. Judging a new opera is perhaps a music critic's hardest task, because all his faculties of mind, eye, and ear are called into play. He must consider the creative aspects of both music and libretto, as well as all the production values previously cited. Whereas in a "standard" opera the production is the thing, and judgment is rarely passed on the music or libretto, the production itself is secondary to a new opera's writing. Yet the production is by no means ignored, and the critic may speculate on how much the opera's success or failure is the result of casting, conductor, director, orchestra, or decor.

As with a classic play or the playing of a rarely heard symphony, the revival of a long-dormant opera warrants discussion of the work's merits today. Has it been unjustly neglected, or has its revival revealed that history's verdict is correct? Why? Has it been revived primarily for its musical values or as a "vehicle" for a reigning prima donna? (It seems that operas are revived only for soprano stars.)

Thus in many ways an operatic rarity is treated as a new work, in discussing the merits of its music and libretto, and in giving the reader a taste of the synopsis. The opera may have been in high fashion in its time, and emerge as a period piece, the work of a lackluster composer. The externals change, the basic values endure. How much of the work is gold and how much is glitter?—a standard that can be applied to any arts creation.

With grand opera, there is also the language.

In Continental Europe, an opera is sung in the language of the country in which it is performed. In England and the United States the opera is usually performed in its original tongue, although better translations and more young American singers are leading to more performances in the vernacular.

There is a never-ending war between opponents and proponents of opera in English. Opponents contend that the native words fit the music uniquely, therefore the music sounds best that way. This is true of a liquid language such as Italian; the "Largo al factotum" from *The Barber of Seville* cannot be sung as speedily in English. When it's a foreign language, you don't have to strain to catch the English words, but need only check on the singers' diction in what may be for them a foreign tongue. Some opera librettos are just as well not sung in English.

Proponents maintain that a listener's enjoyment is increased when he knows what is going on. Any English words caught are that much to the good, and this benefit outweighs any awkwardness in syllabication. The singers may (or may not) feel more at home with the English tongue.

The results may remain inconclusive for years. In New York, Metropolitan Opera audiences have sometimes voted for the Italian to continue, refusing an English translation. The Met on tour has scheduled the same opera in both Italian and English. Across the country it appears that opera in English is gaining headway.

* * *

This review by Harold C. Schonberg, Pulitzer Prize-winning music critic of *The New York Times,* briefly appraises one of Verdi's lesser-known operas but gives most of the attention to the singers and the production. Schonberg rightly feels that it is hardly necessary to go into the synopsis of an opera based on one of Shakespeare's best-known plays.

What with a new conductor and everybody new to his or her role at the Metropolitan Opera, Verdi's "Macbeth" assumed a new look on Thursday evening. It was the first time this season that the opera was given. No matter what one thinks of the Neher production—those costumes! really!—it is a wonderful opera that never fails to make an impact.

And this despite the fact that it was pretty much a failure during Verdi's day and never has been a steady repertory piece. It has no famous arias, no big tenor role and is even a mishmash of styles, because Verdi later worked on it. Yet "Macbeth" grows on one. It's a remarkable example of Verdian drama, and has a strange, brooding quality rare for him in 1847 (the revisions came in 1865). And it has the remarkable sleepwalking scene, a stroke of sheer genius.

It was clear that the Metropolitan Opera had been rehearsing this "Macbeth." The orchestra under Francesco Molinari-Pradelli sounded clean and incisive, and the chorus sang with real pep. A very strong cast was put together, and the result was a "Macbeth" brilliant in song.

The two leading singers were Martina Arroyo and Sherrill Milnes. Miss Arroyo, who looks as though she has lost some weight, applied herself diligently to the role of Lady Macbeth. She continues to improve as an actress, and this role marks a significant step in her development. Miss Arroyo is learning restraint in gesture and movement. She no longer flings her arms out every time she turns, and she has toned down some of her facial expressions.

She was in fine voice Thursday night. If her singing was not uniformly accurate—a few notes were not produced exactly on pitch—it was never less than warm and exciting. Hers is a big, velvety, commanding voice, backed by a solid technique (the trills in the Brindisi were something few contemporary dramatic sopranos attempt), and used in an expressive manner.

In Mr. Milnes she had a partner capable of equal volume and command. He employed his big baritone in a vocally exemplary manner, which means that there were other things in his arsenal than the desire to overpower the audience with high loud notes. There was some smooth legato singing and sometimes a quality of vocal intensity that was not always matched by his acting. Mr. Milnes is a competent but scarcely imaginative actor, and he still has a good deal to go before he can suggest the horror and desperation in the ghost of Banquo scene.

The lesser roles were well done. Ruggero Raimondi as Banquo was admirable. He is one of the smoothest basses before the public, always using his noble voice in a mellifluous manner. And Franco Tagliavini as Macduff delivered his one aria with clarity and spirit. He is a better than average tenor, one with a clearly focused voice and a springy sound. Rod McWherter made the most of his limited opportunities as Malcolm.

Thus this was a superbly sung "Macbeth," and it also was a performance with mounting dramatic tension. Much of this tension came from the pit. Mr. Molinari-Pradelli has at times been less than inspired, but here he was on top of the music, conducting with real strength, never letting the rhythm lag. This performance was what grand opera is all about, and it also brings to the fore one of Verdi's most unusual works. (Copyright *The New York Times*.)

Chapter XVII

FOLK AND ROCK MUSIC

The coming of the microphone permitted the rise of the "popular" singer, the vocalist with the band (in the 1930's and 1940's) of Benny Goodman, Stan Kenton, Sammy Kaye, Ted Lewis, Les Brown, Guy Lombardo, Tommy and Jimmy Dorsey, Glenn Miller. Some of these names still command attention today.

Along with the microphone, an important contribution to pop music was the phonograph record industry, which in the 1970's spread to tapes and cassettes.

Popular music underwent a twofold change in the decade or two after World War II. Anybody who could sing and who bought a guitar, usually with the money he saved on haircuts, became a folk singer.

The term is a broad one. The songs, often original with the performer, are not folk songs in the traditional sense, but topical songs, often of biting wit. From Woody Guthrie to Arlo Guthrie, from Josh White to Joan Baez, the words are usually more important than the music.

The accompaniment may be the singer's own guitar, or the soloist may be backed by several instruments, including piano, drums, string bass, and/or guitar. The lead singer may have a vocal group behind him or her. Occasionally duos or trios, such as Peter, Paul, and Mary, are successful.

The so-called folk music boom that began in the mid-'50's was boosted for the most part by the arrival of the Kingston Trio, which found fantastic commercial success through a slick, polished approach to traditional folk music and newly written "traditional" folk tunes. In time the college crowd—which had been enthusiastic supporters of the Kingston Trio and a few other folk groups that found a certain success (the Journeymen, the Rooftop Singers, and such)—discovered the likes of Joan Baez, who began by singing the "pure" type of folk music and then quickly graduated to the contemporary statement or protest song.

The performance of contemporary folk music has changed in locale, too. Instead of theaters, the folk singers are usually heard in coffee-houses and, in the summer, at outdoor folk and rock festivals, which are dreaded by municipal officials. These festivals attract any number of young people, from a few hundred to the estimated 500,000 at 1969's Woodstock, N.Y.

Because the folk music here described is more folk than music, it can generally be best appreciated by younger reviewers. (Call it the generation gap, or merely cite once more the illustration of strawberry versus vanilla ice cream.) The emphasis, as noted, is on the words rather than the music, but the performer must create a rapport with his audience through the music as well as the words.

How well does he do this? How much of his performance and his sway over his listeners is because of the words, his musical proficiency, or his personal magnetism?

Appraising a folk recital or rock festival may involve more intangibles than any other category of musical performance.

In the early 1950's, rock 'n' roll music was born. It started as the white man's interpretation of the black man's rhythm and blues music. The Memphis influence added country to the rhythm and blues. This brought Elvis Presley into the picture and several others such as Jerry Lee Lewis and Carl Perkins.

Rock—or rockability—drifted around for a year or two without going anywhere in particular, and then came the Beatles and their "Liverpool sound," followed by dozens of other British groups.

The rock scene at the beginning of the Swingin' Seventies was in a continuous flux. First there was the vacuum caused by the defection of the Beatles.

It seemed to this observer that nearly anybody would first pick out a name, then form a group to go with it. (No one had accepted Jackie Gleason's suggestion for the name of a rock group—Uncollected Garbage.)

The term rock 'n' roll itself became outdated. There were subdivisions—hard rock, acid rock—whose meanings were sometimes known only to the initiated. Jack Lloyd, popular-music reviewer of *The Philadelphia Inquirer,* says "they've come up with country-rock, folk-rock, jazz-rock, Bach-rock and, yes, there is even soft-rock."

The Beatles changed not only popular music but male hairdos as well. Here they are seen in a scene from their movie *Help!* Left to right: Paul McCartney, John Lennon, George Harrison, and Ringo Starr. No group could fill their place when they disbanded in 1970.

    Reviewing rock groups requires aural stamina. Some, which keep falling by the wayside, seem to think that the way to overpower the audience is turn up the amplifiers to blast level and pound away.

    Others, such as Chicago, Sly and the Family Stone, the Jefferson Airplane, base their performance on a solid musical—classical—

foundation or training. They have the instrumental technique and the musical imagination to give variety and spice to their playing. There is more to it than a catchy, rhythmic beat.

For this reason the reviewer—young, or over the dreaded age of 30—has some sort of standard by which to judge and on which to write. What makes the group click? What are its strengths and weaknesses? Is it just another so-called rock concert or does the group have something individual to offer?

In addition to the personal and musical criteria listed above for a popular concert, the reviewer should also have in stock a familiarity with the performer's work on records. Rock stars nearly always repeat numbers from their hit records—the audience expects this. Usually some verses are added.

Knowledge of the soloist's or group's song hits is helpful for another reason: There are never any programs at a rock concert. You can write down the numbers or, if you are lucky, get a list of them either before or, more likely, after the show. A cynic may contend that the names of the numbers don't matter—they all sound alike. Regardless, the titles do help in writing the review.

Chapter XVIII

POPULAR AND CLASSICAL MUSIC: SHALL THE TWAIN EVER MEET?—MUSIC BY CHANCE

For decades musicians have been trying to wed classical and popular music. Some, such as composer George Gershwin, bridged the gap in their way. James de Preist, now a rising symphony conductor, put on concerts with both classical and jazz music as a University of Pennsylvania undergraduate; the longhair music usually overshadowed the then shorthair music.

There have been recent and more successful attempts to merge both kinds of longhair music in the concert hall. Composer and pianist Dave Brubeck is a leader here. Conductor Leonard Bernstein gave numerous concerts with jazz ensembles and the New York Philharmonic sharing the stage and playing the same piece or two.

Obviously such concerts feature the classical-music ensemble, which is older, larger, and more powerful. What results?

A mixing of chocolate and vanilla ice cream may produce vanilla fudge. Most ice cream fanciers call the combination tasty, cutting down the strong chocolate effect and enhancing the blander vanilla flavor.

How does a vanilla fudge concert impress you? Are jazz and symphonic elements in tasty proportion? Is this merely a hybrid concert or does it have a character of its own? Does the concert have something to say that could not be as well expressed purely in symphonic or jazz terms?

Then there's music by chance, or aleatory music. Some players may have music entirely written out, others will have a huge expanse of music, and the musician plays whatever section his eye lights on. Thus the music is never heard the same way twice.

Composer John Cage, and Lukas Foss, composer, conductor, and pianist, are pioneers of aleatory music in this country; Karlheinz Stockhausen, of Germany, is its high priest in Europe.

Some conductors also experiment with pure ensemble improvisation: They cue the musicians when to begin and stop playing; otherwise the players are entirely on their own.

These two developments—jazz and chance—are growing and widening. Critics frequenting the concert hall must stretch their outlook. But with a firm foundation of theory and experience, an open-minded reviewer should meet such challenges in stride.

What to look and listen for? Since it's music by chance, one cannot provide many advance signals. One can best reiterate: Check the details, but most of all, appraise the overall effect of the piece or the concert.

Chapter XIX

BALLET AND THE MODERN DANCE

I have tried to avoid technical terms in writing about music reviewing. One does not make music critics in three easy lessons. This book is meant to be only a primer in the practice of reviewing the arts. Aptitude and experience take over from here.

Similarly, one chapter on the dance can serve merely as an introduction. But a few do's and don'ts will not be amiss.

Some criteria used for any art apply to the dance: in creativity—the music, the choreography, and the decor (sets and costumes). In the dance, even more than in opera, the center of attention is visual. And the distinctive part of dance is the choreography, the dance itself.

There are, of course, many kinds of dance. Principal fields today are the classical ballet, of which the Russians are the prime exponents; the modern dance, which in the United States has taken many forms, parallel to the development of modern music; and folk dancing. Naturally they overlap. Large ballet companies with classical orientation present some works in the modern idiom or with a folk flavor; avant-garde dance troupes cannot avoid occasional obeisance to tradition.

Just as music is divided into pure and program music, ballet is divided into abstract works and those with a story (*ballet d'action*). You can enjoy a "program" ballet without knowing the story, but it is helpful to know the synopsis; otherwise, it may be like arriving late at a movie or play.

First, the creative aspects. As in any other art, the critic will not be able to speculate on the originality of the work unless he has some familiarity with the work of other choreographers from Marius Petipa to George Balanchine and Martha Graham, to name but three. He may be less concerned with originality of style than he is with the effectiveness of the choreography, how well it translates into dance and the story it tells.

A play tells a story in words and action, with settings and costumes. An opera adds music and substitutes singing for speech. A program ballet tells a story in pantomime, with music and decor.

Regarding the creative aspects of the program ballet, the reviewer will apply, to the story, many of the criteria of a play or movie. Is the story believable? Is it told well in terms of its medium? Are the principal characters developed credibly? Do the subsidiary characters enhance or impede the story? Character development may take place in a full-length ballet, but in most ballets of fifteen or twenty minutes' duration, there is exposition rather than development.

As to the decor, costumes may play their part, scenery may be a factor, and there will be few if any stage props.

If the ballet is new, the music also must be judged. Has the music been written especially for this work, or has the ballet been set to new or old music? Either way, how well do music and choreography fit? If the music was composed for this ballet, the composer and choreographer may have collaborated so closely that the music and dance seem inseparable. Other ballets, generally abstract ones, may use the work of great composers. Balanchine set his *Concerto Barocco* to Bach's *Two-Violin Concerto,* his *Serenade* to Tchaikovsky's *Serenade for Strings.* Some composers are remembered only for their ballet music, such as Ludwig Minkus. The critic may ponder whether the music, if new, would be worthwhile if it stood alone. (The music of many great ballets is familiar in concert and on records—*Firebird, Nutcracker,* etc. It's worth hearing for its own sake. Not so Minkus' *Don Quixote* or Herman Lovenskjold's *La Sylphide!*) This new ballet music may achieve its prime purpose of enhancing the choreography, but like most movie scores may not be usable otherwise.

The new ballet may be set to old music—probably an accepted masterpiece such as a Bach suite, a Beethoven symphony or movement therefrom, or a collection of short works such as Chopin (*Les Sylphides*) or Tchaikovsky excerpts. The music may be by a composer of lesser worth. In either case, the choreography and the wedding of the dance and music are paramount, but it doesn't hurt to use good music.

As with an old play, the emphasis in the staging of an old ballet is on the performance. The ballet may be a restaging of a favorite, such as *The Sleeping Beauty* or *The Nutcracker.* Are the changes for the better, or at least are they valid? If the troupe presents standard works (usually abstract ones), the criteria are those of the performance itself—Michel Fokine's *Les Sylphides,* Balanchine's *Theme and Variations,* to name but two.

Whether old or new work, whether program or abstract ballet, there are criteria of performance judgment for soloists and corps de

Two top stars of the classical ballet, Rudolf Nureyev and Dame Margot Fonteyn, are shown here in *Swan Lake* in a production of the British Royal Ballet. Nureyev, a defector from Soviet Russia, and Fonteyn, who continued dancing long after the age of 50, have been box-office dynamite whenever they have appeared together.

(PHOTO BY: MIRA)

ballet. The ballet corps may be likened to a chorus or other ensemble. Ensemble—that's the word! Do the dancers of the corps perform together, are their movements synchronized when they are supposed to be (unity of ensemble)? Are the corps dancers sufficiently accomplished individually and can each maintain the pace of the ensemble?

The severest tests for a ballet corps come in some of the traditional ballets such as *Les Sylphides* or *Swan Lake*. Here the ensemble, sometimes divided into two parts on either side of the stage, is expected to perform in perfect unison. The dancers' unity of ensemble may be a measure of the ballet company's ability as a whole.

Then of course there are the solo dancers—the ballerinas, the danseurs nobles (male partners of the ballerinas), and lesser soloists. The balletomane may glory in the use of technical description—entrechats, fouettés, jeté, en pointe, tours, and of course pas de deux. In my ballet reviews I have generally been content to speak of spins, leaps, and turns, feeling (justly or not) that otherwise most daily newspaper readers might not know what I'm talking about.

How well do the solo dancers impress you? Does their dancing—their leaps, spins, and turns—seem labored or effortless? A true ballerina will seem to float in the air; nor will an accomplished male dancer be earthbound. Does the ballerina's partner aid her solos? Do the pair harmonize—are they equal in ability, or is one hampered by the other?

As in opera, the ballet conductor and orchestra must be considered, too. Do the conductor and his dancers have the same idea about tempo, or does the conductor appear to be rushing the dancers or holding them back? Does the orchestra give what is required of it, or are there technical slips?

Modern dance is about as different from classical ballet as twenty-first-century music is from Mozart. Whether the modern ballet professes to tell a story or is avowedly abstract, it may be as hard to figure out as an avant-garde play.

Modern dancers strike this observer as needing even greater control over their bodies than classical dancers. They often assume angular poses that would trouble a professional gymnast.

Since a reviewer will be seeing most modern ballet numbers for the first time, he will usually strive to appraise their creative aspects. And like any new creations, they must be judged on their own terms. What is the modern choreographer trying to convey, either in story form or the abstract? And how well does the performance succeed, both in choreography and in performance?

Do the dancers have sufficient technique for the works at hand? This may be less of en pointe and leaps and turns than bending the body backwards or in pretzel shapes.

Some modern choreography will move the reviewer profoundly,

other numbers will leave him cold. Sometimes he will find himself hard pressed for adequate description; other times—as in reviewing other arts—the words may come tumbling out faster than he can type.

Modern dance has kept pace with the other fine arts—painting, sculpture, music, and drama, not to mention James Joyce. The dedicated arts reviewer will find some of his most stimulating evenings at contemporary dance.

Most dance groups—the term is used in preference to ballet companies—today specialize in the modern dance. Aside from being in tune with the times, their presentations need fewer physical resources. They can be performed by fewer dancers; they need little in settings other than a backdrop; costumes may be as elementary as rehearsal leotards or gym suits; and the music can be taped or played by a small ensemble, rock or otherwise.

Local ballet schools and companies usually further the classical ballet in varying degrees of competency and imagination.

The major companies, such as the New York City Ballet and the Pennsylvania Ballet, attempt the best of both styles. Their choreographers fuse elements of the classical and the modern in new works that may use old or new music. They restage standard works from the classical repertory and introduce new ones to contemporary music. It is a formula that works when there are sufficient resources of creative and performing talent—and money.

The folk dancing reviewed in newspapers is usually that of an exotic troupe brought by Sol Hurok or other impresarios from the Soviet Union, Europe, Mexico, Africa, Israel, India, or the Philippines. Sometimes it is not genuine folk dancing (traditional works that may be hundreds of years old) but virtuosic individual and ensemble display with a folk basis, such as that devised by Moiseyev. The troupes will often bring their own instruments, sometimes singers (?!) too. Instrumental and vocal numbers, without dancers, are not uncommon.

The dazzling dances and beauty of the costumes will sometimes beggar description. The reviewer will often find that superb entertainment is provided, and that he may apply many of the dance criteria previously noted in this chapter. At other times a sense of sameness will be manifest by the end of the program.

The reviewer should strive to assay folk dancing on its own terms as well as from the sophisticated westerner's viewpoint. He should not become emotionally involved with the ethnic or political background of the troupe. The dance, like music, is an international language.

* * *

This review of the Royal Ballet's *Swan Lake* in 1963 marked the Philadelphia debut of Rudolf Nureyev.

His debut, of course, was the major news. But the other dancers and the physical production are not neglected by the reviewer. In general, the inverted-pyramid style is followed in the construction of this article.

At Convention Hall

Fonteyn Soars To New Heights With Nureyev

By Samuel L. Singer

To say that the Royal Ballet put its best foot forward on Thursday would be doing an injustice to the stars who performed on Wednesday at Convention Hall. Nevertheless, it was the top drawing cards of this richly endowed company—Dame Margot Fonteyn and Rudolf Nureyev—who garnered the show-stopping applause in the four-act version of "Swan Lake."

It marked the debut here of Nureyev, 24-year-old Russian star who won international fame when he defected from the Soviets, and who has clinched that fame with his dancing. Tall, handsome, ascetic, he made spectacular leaps and turns seem effortless; apparently he is a ballet astronaut.

His partnering of Dame Margot was equally breath-taking, for the ballerina has perhaps never sailed so high or so securely in the lifts, and Nureyev held her almost aloft to conclude their pas de deux in Act 3.

Nureyev brought dramatic force to his portrayal of Prince Siegfried, who must choose a bride. Miss Fonteyn was lightness itself in dancing the twin roles of Odette-Odile, under the spell of the evil magician. It is hard to believe she first danced this part 25 years ago.

"Swan Lake" was not only a spectacle in its physical production, with lavish sets and lovely costumes, but it served to display the amazing resources in number of leading dancers this company has.

Where one company may be glad to have one dozen swans in the famous second act, this company has two dozen. Like the Metropolitan and a few other opera companies, where leading singers may assume secondary roles, here all the parts were filled by first-line dancers.

The various characteristic dances, pas de six and other ensembles, were all beautifully performed, and it would be like a catalogue to offer individual encomiums. But mention must be made, of course, of the Cygnets who danced as one: Maureen Maitland, Margaret Lyons, Jacqueline Haslam and Virginia Wakelyn.

Other leading roles were well taken by Stanley Holden, as the amusing Tutor; Derek Rencher, as Benno, the Prince's friend; Leslie Edwards, the magician (hiss-s-s!), and Gerd Larsen as the Prince's Mother.

John Lanchbery conducted the Tchaikovsky score with both gusto and accuracy. Leslie Hurry's eye-filling decor complemented the Petipa-Ivanov choreography as revised by Ninette de Valois, retiring director of the company.

* * *

Here is a later production of the same company's *Swan Lake* that Clive Barnes, most famous and probably the best informed of any newspaper critic for ballet, did not like.

Notice the reviewer's use of paradoxical pairings of words such as "cheaply expensive."

For those who do not have an unabridged dictionary, "niveous" means snowy or snowlike. I do not think a reviewer should send even readers of *The New York Times* to the dictionary.

Poor Start Is Overcome in Later Scenes

Dance: 'Swan Lake' by Royal Ballet

By Clive Barnes

Vice can as easily be taken for granted as virtue. The fact is the despair of moralists the world over. Now that we have become so accustomed to the glaring faults and more marginal infelicities of the Royal Ballet's current production of Tchaikovsky's "Swan Lake," there is a temptation to take them in our stride. It is, like few temptations, one to be resisted.

This is a German-opera-house-style production of "Swan Lake," drearily embelished with cheaply expensive designs by Carl Toms, with only its great remnants of past glories and the quality of its actual performance to belatedly commend it. It is a production that should not so much be amended as changed altogether.

The ballet opened sadly. Sir Frederick Ashton's normally corruscating pas de quatre looked dispirited, with only Michael Coleman putting up a losing battle against his colleagues, and even Rudolf Nureyev, most eloquent of all Prince Siegfrieds, took his own first solo too impulsively for its true legato feel. And then came Monica Mason's Odette, and, fundamentally, all was well. With an Odette such as this the production takes second place. This was lovely dancing, crystal-clean, outline sketched in the purest snow, sharp yet fugitive.

Here in this second act Ivanov's choreography is preserved intact, and it was very pleasant to see the restoration of the original duet for the Leading Swans in place of the previously interpolated quartet originally in this production. And here the entire beauty of the Royal Ballet's old "Swan Lake" reasserted itself, with the ensemble dancing with that poetic precision that has been its hallmark this season, Mr. Nureyev, an archetypally ardent Siegfried, and Miss Mason the most sensuous and niveous of Odettes.

The Ballroom scene, which looks like an unsuccessfully grandiose restaurant in Mr. Toms' aggressively vulgar setting, is less happy. Yet this featured some marvelous dancing, notably by Lesley Collier and Alexander Grant in the Neapolitan Dance (one of Ashton's choreographic gems) and, of course, Miss Mason and Mr. Nureyev in the Black Swan pas de deux.

Miss Mason's Odette is imperious—a veritable Queen of the Swans—and, expectedly, her twin portrait of the false Odile continues the regal image, but here with an air of flamboyant evil rather than tragic doom. Her dancing lacks something in pure classic line. It has not the clarity of a classic ballerina, but more the total involvement of a dramatic ballerina, yet this is more a noting of interpretation than an adversely critical comment.

Mr. Nureyev danced with that special quality of awareness that is almost his alone. He sees the classic dance as a tightrope walk against disaster. I think it was Schiller who demanded that the artist dare death. That is the greatness of Nureyev. He puts himself on the line.

* * *

Although it's *Les Sylphides* and Tchaikovsky that sell ballet tickets, the news of this performance was the local premiere, so the reviewer (who had plenty of space that edition) devoted the core of his article to describing the choreography, the music, and the dancing of the new work. The two older works are described succinctly.

At Convention Hall

'Elektra' Provides a Shocker

By Samuel L. Singer

The kind of bread matters, but it's the filling that makes the sandwich. And sandwiched between the bland virtuosity of "Les Sylphides" and spectacle of "Aurora's Wedding," the Royal Ballet gave the local premiere of "Elektra" Wednesday. This shocker provided the meat of the evening.

Perhaps ballet ticket-buyers are like symphony subscribers. New works are necessary—to some a necessary evil—but it's Beethoven, Brahms and Tchaikovsky that sell the tickets.

That seems to be the prevalent feeling among concert managers, but rather than the oft-repeated "Les Sylphides" and "Aurora's Wedding," this non-ticket-buyer would have preferred another one or two of the Royal Ballet's new works.

The ballet was transferred from its original Academy of Music booking to Convention Hall, and this hall has several advantages besides larger capacity (ticket prices at the Academy would have been much higher). The larger stage allows full scope for the Royal Ballet's sweeping, often spectacular scenery. And the hall is air-conditioned.

"Elektra," the horror-drenched Grecian tragedy which may have given Lizzie Borden her ideas, was danced with the same four principals who created the roles at Covent Garden last March 26. These were Nadia Nerina in the title part, David Blair as her brother Orestes, Monica Mason as Clytemnestra, their mother, and Derek Rencher as Aegisthus, Clytemnestra's lover, now king.

The Dali-like backdrop and sidedrops designed by Arthur Boyd portray futuristic faces, limbs and bodies, perfectly complementing the music by Malcolm Arnold.

The music is stridently discordant at first, and through much of the ballet, although it becomes momentarily gentler as Orestes returns to Elektra.

Both the music and choreography build up suspense when Elektra seizes that long ax and urges Orestes to action to avenge their father's murder.

The ballet is a scant 15 minutes long, but they are memorable minutes. It was superbly danced by the principals and by eight men as the omnipresent Erinyes whose curse haunts the family.

The pageantry of "Aurora's Wedding," the third act of Tchaikovsky's "Sleeping Beauty," exerted its customary spell, as each fairy-tale duo or trio triumphed.

But the most thrilling steps were by Donald Macleary as the Prince and Svetlana Beriosova in the title role. Their leaps, spins and figurations, singly and together, won the evening's biggest cheers.

These two also starred in "Les Sylphides," to Chopin music and Fokine's choreography, wherein the corps de ballet proved its unexcelled precision.

Robert Irving conducted all three ballets expertly.

Chapter XX

BOOK REVIEWING

The principles of play and movie reviewing apply to book reviewing: You want a readable lead and you characterize the nature of the book with a minimum of synopsis. You appraise the writing: Is it vivid or dull? Does it carry the reader along or is it plodding?

A book review should get the space it merits through the volume's news value—the importance of the author, the newsworthiness of the book and what the author has to say.

In a work of fiction, is the plot convincing? Does it have originality? Is the style the author's own or is it influenced by Joyce (naturalism), Hemingway (realism), Saroyan (naiveté), or anyone else? Young writers are often influenced subconsciously.

Are the characters lifelike? Are they developed three-dimensionally? You may describe the principal and subsidiary characters much as you describe those in a play. Occasionally an outstanding passage demands quotation. David Appel, retired book editor of *The Philadelphia Inquirer,* says that synopsis should not be more than 25 percent of a review. The rest, except for the facts of authorship and publication, should be analysis and qualitative appraisal.

Some reviewers underline pertinent passages as they read. Others write down such passages or make page references on file cards that may be easily arranged at review-writing time.

In nonfiction, you quote as space permits to illustrate the author's main points. The author's position and ideas should be clearly communicated, although you may disagree with them. Quotations should enlighten the reader.

In some ways, the review of a nonfiction work may be compared to the "block form" of reporting speeches—indirect, summary quotes alternating with direct, illustrative quotes.

The author may or may not need identification. If possible, you may wish to compare this new work with others by the same author, or by others in the nonfiction field. However, the review of the present work should be paramount.

Appel offers a piece of advice to book reviewers: Do not read the jacket; it may influence you subconsciously.

The fact that the book is the choice of a book club may be a matter of news, but should not influence your judgment of the work. "Book clubs are primarily for selling books by mail, not for the promotion of literature," says Appel. "They may widen readership,

Nobel Prize-winning author Pearl S. Buck, who died in 1973 at the age of 80, also won fame as a humanitarian for her wide-ranging efforts to aid Asian-American children.

but may have a deleterious effect on American writing because they subtly influence authors to write on formula. Intelligent readers should be wary of hand-picked books. Other books are worth reading, too."

The book clubs have had an enormous influence on American writers and publishers. A book's selection by a club increases the chances of its sale to films. The clubs are the biggest monetary factor in publishing today; sometimes a single sale to a book club has saved a publisher.

A further suggestion, applicable to reviewers of plays and movies as well: Do not be flippant. Avoid smart phrases designed for quotation in ads.

* * *

This review of an award-winning novelist's latest book talks less of the plot than of the author's distinctive style. It also draws some comparisons with the novelist's previous works.

"The Devil Tree," by Jerzy Kosinski. Harcourt Brace, $6.95
By Larry Swindell
Book editor of *The Philadelphia Inquirer*

From Joseph Conrad to Vladimir Nabokov, acquaintance with authors for whom English is an adopted language is a tantalizing detour on the literary roadmap; you encounter scenery you'd never notice on the main highway. Somehow these writers illuminate the language more knowingly than those born to it. Jan de Hartog, another exemplary second-language novelist, once told me that English is both the most musical and pictorial language, but easily abused by its complacent natives. This contention is validated resoundingly by the Polish-born Jerzy Kosinski, who now has written four novels in English. With Kosinski, style becomes distillation itself. Every syllable functions toward a rhythm and cadence that stimulates reading; and the imagery is so vivid as to purge any possible ambiguity.

Yet the heartbeat of Kosinski's fiction is not style but substance. If Nabokov evokes a purple-mountained majesty above de Hartog's fruited plain, then Jerzy Kosinski lures us into a darkling forest and enthralls us with the shrubbery of his peculiar pessimism. Now the foliage includes the baobab, or "devil tree": its branches seem to be roots, and its roots the branches.

Heretofore Kosinski has implicated the evil inherent in mankind, but I believe he means the devil tree to symbolize specifically the contemporary American malaise. Jonathan Whalen, his focal character ("hero" is an inadmissible term) is ensnared by its roots, and they are choking him to spiritual death. Whalen is sole heir to one of the world's great industrial fortunes. He consumes the American Dream and then vomits it—the rich boy who has everything and who has nothing.

God knows he tries to find something tangible: opium in Burma, whoremongering around the world; nothing lasts. Whalen is one passive playboy almost monumentally vague, although he exhibits a remarkable ingenuity when he accomplishes a double murder in another futile effort to cure his mysterious ailment of emptiness. Finally he flips out. It can't sound pleasant. It isn't. But try to keep from reading every page, and then be careful: Jonathan Whalen's trance becomes your own.

The body of Kosinski's work, both fiction and nonfiction, reveals a consuming interest in "dead souls" and no literary soul is quite so dead as Jonathan Whalen's. Is there hope for the Whalens of the world and, indeed, is there hope for us all? I am not disturbed that Kosinski isn't answering this question, but I'm rankled that most critics don't seem to realize he's asking it.

The critical establishment that hailed Kosinski's advent with "The Painted Bird" and then tapped him for the National Book Award for "Steps" began to take him to task two years ago with "Being There" (I thought it brilliant) and now they are flailing him anew. There's a consensus of dissatisfaction with Kosinski's harrowing view of humanity, and some clear annoyance that he is not developing as a novelist along orthodox lines. "The Devil Tree" does not conform to the classic narrative unities, and is an anthology of impressionistic fragments from Jonathan Whalen's pitiable life.

"The Painted Bird" was Kosinski's most nearly conventional novel in form if not content and may still be his finest achievement; but I suspect Kosinski finds little fascination for conventionality or the best-seller list. He's a vital, committed social critic; and if he believes the world is stuck with a pretty sorry human race, he may also believe that society itself is salvageable. But only possibly.

* * *

This review of an autobiography briefly describes the subject but otherwise lets this "British Tom Dewey" speak for himself.

"The Art of the Possible": The Memoirs of Lord Butler
Gambit, $10.00
By Steve Neal

When British voters rejected Winston Churchill's Conservative Party after World War II, Richard Austin Butler convinced Tory leaders to "wrest the initiative in the realm of political ideas from the left" by adopting a progressive social policy.

He built a new image for the party, coining such slogans as "Property-Owning Democracy" and "Humanizing, not Nationalizing Industry."

As a result of Butler's strategy the Conservatives returned to power in 1951, but many of his colleagues regarded him as a "pink conservative."

Such ideological fears undoubtedly contributed to his failure to win election as Prime Minister. So did his personality. Tall, scholarly, and unassertive, many people regarded him as cold and aloof.

During Butler's 35-year political career he served as Foreign Secretary, Deputy Prme Minister, Chancellor of the Exchequer, Minister of Education, and Minister of Labor.

On three occasions he was a favorite to become Prime Minister. Instead he is Britain's most famous also-ran, Thomas Dewey with a dry wit.

Unlike contemporaries Harold Macmillan and Anthony Eden, Butler decided against writing multi-volume memoirs. He "preferred a single book which is not too heavy for anyone to hold up and doze over in bed."

The book is autobiography at its best—occasionally self-effacing, always perceptive, revealing, and authoritative.

Of Neville Chamberlain's Munich settlement, Butler writes: "The critics of Munich, though deserving on all respects, persevere in passion by denying its historical inevitability."

Munich should be remembered as a ". . . pause, however inglorious, which enabled Churchill when his time came to lead the nation through the valley of the shadow to victory."

Butler recalls Churchill's eleventh-hour endorsement of Macmillan in 1957: "I had served Churchill for ten years, four as his Chancellor, but he told me later 'I went for the older man'." Churchill, though recognizing Butler's talents, never forgot his loyalty to Chamberlain after Munich.

Of the Suez crisis, Butler says Prime Minister Eden made a fatal mistake in branding Nasser a fascist. Butler notes that Egypt's government "represented a popular movement, not an imposed tyranny."

Of the 1963 defeat when his election as Prime Minister seemed a certainty, Butler discusses Macmillan's opposition: "I think that Harold always had a feeling, despite the nine years between us, that my succession would not make enough difference between his regime and the next."

In 1965 Butler was appointed life peer and master of Trinity College in Cambridge. At 70 he takes comfort from the fact that his postwar policies, with only minor deviation, continue to govern Britain's domestic affairs. (Reprinted from *The Philadelphia Inquirer*)

* * *

The reviewer is drama and motion picture critic for *The Philadelphia Inquirer*. Although no critic can possibly entirely agree with another critic, his enthusiasm for Miss Kael's anthology is evident, despite questioning of some of her judgments.

The headline on this review read: "If Her Zest Zigs, Her Zeal Zags."

"Deeper into Movies," by Pauline Kael. Atlantic-Little Brown, $12.95

By William B. Collins

If Pauline Kael weren't so entertaining a critic, one would be tempted to suggest she missed her vocation. She would make a terrific Avon lady. She has a heavy finger on the doorbell. She pushes her line single-mindedly, refusing to take maybe for an answer. Consumer resistance is a paper tiger for her.

Better let her in. She's more fun than anybody we know. Besides, we don't have to buy everything she's selling, do we?

"Deeper into Movies" is Miss Kael's fifth book of collected criticism. The pieces here all come from The New Yorker magazine, in whose pages she holds forth six months of every year. Whatever Miss Kael does during the other six months, her readers need time for rest and recreation. Miss Kael never seems to write at anything less than peak energy. She doesn't give off sparks, she is propelled by them, like a pinwheel.

The essays extend from September 27, 1969 to March 25, 1972, lively years for movies, with plenty enough nonsense to keep a critic wary. While some of us were gingerly trying to get with the "youth movie" phenomenon, Miss Kael saw the ripoff element in it, tagged it as exploitation of the American students' radicalized political consciousness and objected to the "glib 'statements' and cheap sex jokes, the zooming shooting and shock cutting of TV commercials, plus a lot of screaming and ketchup on the lenses."

And yet, she fell for "M*A*S*H," one of the more objectionable of the "now" films. Consistency is not for Miss Kael, whose strength as a film critic is precisely that she is not anchored to any aesthetic, movies being a too variable and vital form of expression to be confined by anyone's poetics.

Miss Kael has other virtues. She never forgets that movies are made for

Book Reviewing 125

commercial as well as artistic reasons, and she can take that in stride, even congratulating "Bob & Carol & Ted & Alice" for its candor—"the acrid commercial flavor is right there, out front."

Miss Kael is no snob. She goes to movies looking for enjoyment and her enthusiasm for the medium is contagious. She is a movie fan (not a "buff") with brains and a sensibility that reacts in an overwhelming way to anything she sees on the screen, good, bad or different.

Although she rarely gets beyond good sense, as she did last fall in her famous review of "Last Tango in Paris," Miss Kael can praise a film unreservedly and make the praise stick. Her essay on "The Godfather" leaves very little to be said about that film's superior qualities. The Kael treatment of "McCabe and Mrs. Miller" is a model of appreciation in depth. And she is not ashamed to admit that Frederick Wiseman's documentary, "Hospital," made her cry.

Until her effusion over "Last Tango," though, Miss Kael's fate wasn't much different from any other critic's. It's the pans that the public remembers, to the point where the term "criticism" has come to mean brickbats in the popular mind. Miss Kael does very well in this line, too.

"Song of Norway" is dismissed in a phrase—"second-generation kitsch"—while the cop-out of "Patton" gets an extended and devastating analysis. The brutality of the film version of Harold Robbins' "The Adventurers" provokes some withering thoughts on the coarsening effects of violence on the screen.

Unfortunately, some of Miss Kael's better hatchet jobs are done on grounds which seem almost willfully perverse. Her greatest weakness is a literal-mindedness of the kind that leads her to draw a strained comparison between Fellini's "Satyricon" and the schlock paganism of Cecil B. DeMille or to object to Ken Russell's "Music Lovers" because the movie plays fast and loose with the facts of Tchaikovsky's life.

With this distrust of imagination in its freer flights, Miss Kael makes some very strange judgments on musicals. She is immune to the charm of "The Boy Friend" but entirely happy with the stolid, pedestrian pleasures of "Fiddler on the Roof."

Although Miss Kael's busy, darting, assured manner allows for no backtalk, you nevertheless find yourself arguing with her. And you will find it impossible to read her book straight through, even if she wanted you to. You simply have to get away from her occasionally. Go to the corner saloon, have a drink with the boys, take a walk, do anything. Ignore her for a while. She won't mind. She'll be waiting for you when you get back. She knows you will come back.

Chapter XXI

RECORD REVIEWING

As with any other medium of performance—stage, film, television—many general comments, previously made, apply here, but certain factors are unique to recordings.

Technical perfection, as to performance, may be achieved through repeated "takes" and the fact that a single word or note may be spliced into the tape. The ministrations of producers and sound engineers, the placing of microphones, balancing, and the mixing of soundtracks into the finished product are among the factors that help differentiate a recording from a live performance.

Generally, record producers say they strive for what they call "concert-hall realism," although actually their goal is to make the recording sound best on a home phonograph. And their success in this matter is usually a prime criterion of the record reviewer.

The technical perfection achieved through careful tape editing may sometimes rob a performance of spontaneity and urgency. These qualities may be more apparent in a recording made from a live concert-hall or theater performance (or several performances), even though a few technical imperfections are heard—along with the audience applause and perhaps coughs or laughs.

At any rate, the reviewer of records, tapes, or cassettes tries to assay the effectiveness of the performance—play, musical, poetry, essay, rock or folk concert, musical composition, or whatever (this last category is broad!)—in terms of the record or tape medium. Presumably he has good sound-reproducing equipment on which to listen. He checks for proper balance of voices and instruments, for "presence," for surface noise, or other intrusion of extraneous sound.

He checks for realism and balance. Stereo generally provides a better, more realistic reproduction of a stage show, opera, or other musical event involving more than one performer. Does the stereo recording seem natural or does the performance bounce from one

Record Reviewing

German baritone Dietrich Fischer-Diekau has made more recordings than any classical artist in history. Here he is shown at home with pianist Gerald Moore, perhaps the most famous contemporary accompanist.

(DEUTSCHE GRAMMOPHON PHOTO)

speaker to the other? In other words, does stereo enhance a performance, as it should, or is stereo used as a gimmick?

Some manufacturers have taken historic recordings, made by Toscanini and other greats of the past, and applied the stereophonic process to recordings that were originally monophonic. Does this aid the aural result?

Few monophonic recordings are being made now. But when possible, the reviewer should listen to both monophonic and stereo and comment on both for his readers. Occasionally, as with a piano recital, the monophonic record may be better.

Recordings are one field in which comparisons are not only advisable, but are a necessity for greatest service to your readers. The reviewer of a stage show or movie can tell his readers whether or not to see this show. A record reviewer should comment not only on the quality of the performance at hand, but how it stacks up to others of the same work (particularly those available in the current Schwann catalogue). Most music-lovers buy only one recording of a work, whereas some collectors will acquire every available recording of a favorite opera, ensemble, or individual classical or popular artist.

If your reader does not own the work being reviewed, he may want (or not want) to buy this new recording upon your recommendation. If he does own it, he is still interested in how his copy rates in comparison to the new one.

A recording is a combination of interpretive skill and sound reproduction. Many times a reviewer will hear an excellent interpretation that is marred by deficient reproduction. Perhaps oftener, he will note a poor interpretation dressed up in sound that is breathtakingly reproduced. Always he will have the problem of balancing interpretative and phonographic factors in making recommendations to his readers.

Just as much as in the live performing arts, reviewing records demands taste and background. A serious record reviewer will eventually find that his living quarters are becoming crowded by shelves upon shelves of records. He is glad to dispose of records not worth keeping, but performances that have one or another outstanding factor find room on his shelves, until he has half a dozen recordings of *Carmen, The Barber of Seville,* Beethoven's *Fifth Symphony, Hamlet,* and *The Merry Widow.*

An occupational hazard of the record reviewer is that he may become too engrossed in records and neglect performances in the theater and concert hall. He should always remember that recordings spring from live performances. Continuing attendance at shows and musical events will keep his mind refreshed and help maintain his sense of proportion.

* * *

This roundup of piano recordings covers half a dozen keyboard artists and their various styles of playing. Few direct comparisons with other recordings are made, but the article by Daniel Webster, music critic of *The Philadelphia Inquirer,* reads easily.

John Ogdon has ranged widely in the piano repertory, recording music from Busoni to Tippett to Beethoven. In his latest album he collects diabolical music by Liszt, those shorter pieces that seem charged with demonic fire (Seraphim 60170).

The music is showy, but Ogdon's playing is not shallow and merely flashy. For all his ability to call up round tones, his playing is anchored in precise rhythmic progress inflected by a knowing rubato. The familiar "Mephisto Waltz" is dusted off once more, but Ogdon goes on to a titanic reading of "Funerailles" and some remarkable technical wizardry in "Csardas Macabre."

The Transcendental Etude No. 2, the Prelude and March for a Funeral and "En Rêve" complete the disk. "Funerailles" remains in the ears from this reading, however, since Ogdon finds the way to keep building and building beyond what listeners expect from the piano.

Lili Kraus continues her exploration of Schubert (Vanguard 10074) with the Sonata in A, Opus 120, and the A-minor Sonata, Opus 42.

Her playing is highly personal, songful, freely phrased, highly romantic in the best sense. The freedoms she allows herself are apt in these ample, flowing works.

She is at her best in the melodically simple slow movements, displaying her fine sense of line and ability to sustain that even mood.

RCA has reissued performances from the mid-50s by Wanda Landowska (VIC 1535). Playing a piano, she recorded the Mozart Sonata in D (K. 311) and the Haydn Andante and Variations in F minor.

She managed to make her piano sound like the light-voiced, crisp instruments Mozart knew, not the stentorian grands. Her playing mixed the scholar's concern for correct ornamentation with a romanticist's unhesitating ability to linger on a phrase ending. A highly individual performance, but one which captures, willy nilly, the spirit of the music and its force.

A golden reading of the Schumann Concerto is out by Sviatoslav Richter (DGG 2538025). The pianist plays with flexibilty, a superb and varied tone and sense of tempo that convinces. If the Warsaw Philharmonic were as subtle in accompaniment, this would be the one version to own, but Witold Rowicki's support is pallid. It is almost as if the orchestra could not hear the wonders Richter was working at the keyboard.

On the other side, Mstislav Rostropovich plays the Schumann Cello Concerto with the Leningrad Philharmonic. Here the orchestra is up to the level of the soloist. Rostropovich creates a vast range of sound in what is an inchoate piece of orchestral writing, and the orchestra echoes his range. Gennadi Rozhdestvensky conducts.

Liszt is receiving continued attention by recording companies. Herbert von Karajan conducts four works in an album titled "Fireworks" that is just that, but it also includes a performance by pianist Shura Cherkassky (DGG 2538077).

The Hungarian Fantasy gets the full treatment, flashing piano, searing orchestral playing, showy emotions and moods. Cherkassky makes a brave show in the Fantasy, arguing for its power with hands that command a big sound.

Karajan conducts the Berlin Philharmonic in the Hungarian Rhapsodies Nos. 2, 4 and 5, completing what is an outing for the Berlin Pops.

Emil Gilels played a Mozart program here last fall and has recorded most of that recital (DGG 2530061) during a performance at the Mozarteum in Salzburg.

He proved a sensitive and probing Mozart player in recital and those qualities are apparent here. He plays with a warm sound, but not at the expense of clear lines or scholarly ornamentation. The record collects two Sonatas, in B minor (K. 281) and D minor (K. 310), the Fantasie in D minor (K. 397) and the Variations on Paisiello's "Salve Tu, Domine" (K. 398). The Fantasie is the best in a fine disk.

Artur Rubinstein's tapes have been combed for "The Chopin I Love," newly published (RCA 4000). The pianist's essential joyful playing comes through in this collection, and for the person looking for a summary of Rubinstein's style, this is it. Included are the Polonaise in A flat, the "Minute" Waltz, and familiar Nocturnes, Waltzes and the G-minor Ballade.

Chapter XXII

ART CRITICISM

Probably nowhere in the arts forms is the field so bewildering as in the fine arts themselves—painting and sculpture. A background in art is possibly more necessary here than in the performing arts, yet paradoxically some modern art may be reviewed with little or no background.

For one thing, Marcel Duchamp's definition of art as "anything in an art context" (gallery or museum) no longer suffices. Sculpture abounds in front of office buildings, in parks, and in homes. And, in or out of art museums, are "things" that except by definition of their creators are not art at all in the previously accepted sense.

One artist may paint an absolutely white square and hang it in a museum. A sculptor may weld two pieces of steel, and may give it a title or not. Then of course there is Andy Warhol's Pop art, a magnified Campbell Soup can, for example.

Artists and the public have swept aside objective critical standards. This, says critic Barbara Rose, has placed "the modern critic in the odd position of a judge with no laws he can consult for a verdict."*

Yet the art critic, more so than with the performing arts, may utilize the formula given in Chapter V—material, form, and workmanship—as a reasonably objective standard in appraising works of so-called modern or Pop art. Here, as with other arts, the critic may ask himself: What is the artist trying to do (or say) and how well does he do it?

Instead of working in abstracts he can deal in concrete terms. He can name the materials, try to analyze the form, and qualify the workmanship. It can be a workable process.

Canvas is no longer the only surface for painters. Marble and bronze are no longer the only materials for sculptors. Moreover, the line between painting and sculpture is sometimes blurred. A painter today doesn't always use a paintbrush on cloth. He may take odds

---
* *New York* Magazine, March 3, 1969.

and ends from the woods or the rubbish heap and use spray guns on them. The sculptor may work with time-honored materials or he may use plastics, welded steel pieces, wood, foam rubber, or a combination thereof, and may paint over the entire objet d'art.

The materials and the form are on display. Where today's critical judgment comes into play is in the matter of originality and workmanship. Who was the first to bronze baby shoes? Whose idea was it to substitute cubes for circles? Who first used spray paint on flotsam and jetsam and sold the results to art connoisseurs?

The imagination and quality of workmanship in art may still be judged by a harassed critic. The background is most helpful in detecting originality. Is this the artist's own idea or is he following in the path of Picasso, Duchamp, the Dadaists, Matisse, Cézanne, Seurat, Degas, Brancuşi, or someone earlier or later? Like Shakespeare and Bach, the artist may use a previous practitioner's idea and give it new horizons and new force.

Dadaism and Surrealism are two kinds of art that have some common properties of style, and many common denominators of character, iconography, and intent. Duchamp and Arp were Dadaists, Miró a surrealist, for example.

Except for portrait painters, trained academic realists, and the growing ranks of "new realists" who include unconventional realists and photo-realists, those who practice realistic art today as opposed to nonobjective or abstract are usually amateurs. Critics attending exhibits by new artists must perforce broaden their own standards.

Yet it is the exhibitions by such artists as Van Gogh, Renoir, and Picasso that draw long lines of viewers to art museums. In this way the principal roles of the music critic and the art critic are reversed. Although the music critic has much new music to judge, most of his reviews deal with performance of old music. The art critic seldom has an opportunity to write about "old" paintings and sculpture, although times are changing, and nineteenth-century Americana is coming to the fore, as well as some of the long-obscure European schools.

Impressionists and Old Master prices have gone sky-high, forcing people's attention in other directions. American eighteenth- and nineteenth-century painting and sculpture have greatly benefited from this situation, points out Victoria Donohoe, art critic of *The Philadelphia Inquirer*. Thus the upsurge of interest in things American.

Art Criticism

When an exhibit by an acknowledged master arrives, or when his local museum acquires an expensive masterpiece, the art critic should interpret these "standard" works for his readers. Why are they masterpieces? What's so wonderful about them? Here is where his study of the history of art, his background, his knowledge of art prior to the twentieth century serve him in good stead.

Just as a music critic should be able to delineate the fine points of a concert to his readers, an art critic should be able to write why an artist is great, why a painting or sculpture is great. Here, as in writing about the other arts, the details make the difference.

It goes without saying that an art critic should be able to distinguish between an etching, a print, and a lithograph; water color, wash, and gouache; glass, stone, concrete, wood, or plastic, and how oil looks on these various materials.

Is the artist consistent in his execution? One work will usually stand out in an exhibition; others may be judged in relation to it.

Dorothy Grafly, retired art critic of the Philadelphia *Bulletin*, offers this suggestion concerning impressionistic paintings: Take the whole picture in at first glance. Shut your eyes, open them suddenly, and write about your first instantaneous impression.

Are the artist's methods and style—his signature—his own or a forgery?

"The artist is not as interested in criticism as you may think," says Miss Grafly. "If he is a man of integrity, he is satisfied with his work.

"Too many critics use the work of art as an excuse to write a personal essay, instead of dealing with the work of art itself," a fault often seen in the work of young reviewers in class and in underground publications.

* * *

This review of a landmark exhibit of a foremost American realist painter tells of his place in today's American art scene, and contrasts him with others, both before and now. The writer is art critic of *The Philadelphia Inquirer*.

By Victoria Donohoe

No doubt about it, the Andrew Wyeth exhibition at the Pennsylvania Academy of the Fine Arts lives up to expectations as his most comprehensive show anywhere to date. These 222 temperas, watercolors, dry brush and drawings outnumber by 79 the works shown four years ago at Albright-Knox Gallery, Buffalo—till now his largest exhibit. Here are 57 paintings in his principal medium, egg tempera on a gesso panel, compared with a previous high of 47—and 13 of them were done since 1962. If you saw Wyeth's Buffalo show, just over half of it is represented here, and then tripled by the addition of other material, while several of the newest examples are displayed publicly for the first time. It is a handsome exhibit, rather overwhelming, and offers many surprises, even for those who thought they knew the work of the Chadds Ford artist quite well.

Andrew Wyeth's biography is so widely known, we will not go into its details here, except to say that he was born in Pennsylvania in 1917, and during the 1950s became the most successful painter of his generation, paradoxically, when abstraction was the dominant trend of the times. Here was a contemporary realist painter with roots deep in such 19th-century American art tradition as Winslow Homer's themes and the precise detail of our American primitives, who wanted the object or subject he painted to become the all-important thing.

Meanwhile, as people began wondering whether such methods were outworn or still viable, Wyeth continued to flourish away from the crowd, in isolation, painting only the things he has known for a lifetime —nearly always people and places of strong and distinctive character. In the winter his themes are the mills, forges and houses that remain from Chadds Ford's remote and once-great 18th-century industrial center. Then each summer, he goes off to Maine and paints the rugged coastal islands and peninsulas of a landscape evidently so much more familiar to most Americans than our nearby Brandywine Creek region.

Is Wyeth too literal, or is he the greatest living exponent of a long realist tradition? This is a difficult question to answer confidently, even with all the evidence presented by such a wide-ranging show as this. We note that, by inheritance and training, Wyeth possesses an extraordinary technical skill which has served him well in achieving, not what one might expect—academic work—but something genuinely creative and personal as well as representational. Edgar P. Richardson of Winterthur Museum, in an excellent exhibit catalogue, besides pinpointing chronology and clearly distinguishing between watercolor, dry brush and the various drawing techniques, has divided Wyeth's pictures into three distinct phases. Since the last one is the least familiar, it is amply demonstrated here.

First, there are the swift, expressionist watercolors that go back to 1938, but Wyeth soon took up the exacting medium of tempera painting, which he learned from his brother-in-law Peter Hurd, because he liked its dryness, precision, and possible effects both of depth and strong pattern. Wyeth says he regards technical means not as an end in itself, but only the beginning. His early temperas, firm in design and decorative, are especially plentiful here. Albrecht Dürer was becoming his favorite old master, and soon he would discover Rembrandt's drawings. One of the strengths of this exhibit is its generous inclusion of preliminary studies made for most of the major tempera paintings here, which in their final form conceal the process of execution.

Likewise we note, in the second phase of his work which begins after 1945, a new austerity and sharpness of perception, first observed here in the tempera "Kuerner's Hill." Along about 1952, Wyeth began exhibiting dry brush watercolor, a "new" method, carefully thought out and solid, that appealed to his temperament and which he was to develop at very great lengths thereafter. These are done both in his studio and outdoors, and he regards them as a means of "carrying watercolor a little further."

One of these, "The Drifter" of 1964, marks the beginning of the current phase of Wyeth's production. The present period is characterized by an intense interest in life-size portraiture, in which the sitters no longer turn away from the beholder. His vision is quite direct, yet his people lose none of the old poignancy, and there are even occasional tendencies toward picturesqueness. All the facts are here, and Andrew Wyeth respects them. We doubt if this superb exhibit will make the gifted Chester County artist many new enemies in the modern camp, but it is likely to gather countless new admirers among persons awaiting an opportunity to view one of the largest, most thoroughgoing and impressive solo painting exhibits in recent memory.

* * *

Here *The Philadelphia Inquirer* art critic looks at one of the many new phases in modern art. She does it with an open mind while touching on contemporary trends.

By Victoria Donohoe

And now it's "Impossible" art. Philadelphia happens to be the adopted home of one of the world's best-known "Impossible" or "Casual" artists, a proponent of "The New Esthetics." So sooner or later it had to happen—flamboyant Rafael Ferrer is having a one-man show at our town's vanguard showcase, the Institute of Contemporary Art of the University of Pennsylvania, S.W. corner 34th and Walnut sts. (Sept. 25–Oct. 30). It is the largest solo to date for this 38-year-old Puerto Rican sculptor-teacher, younger brother of the actor José Ferrer. And it anticipates by three months Rafael's solo at New York's Whitney Museum.

His show examines a new tendency—some might call it a style—which is beginning to use the materials, the processes and scale of heavy industry, of technology, our natural environment and sometimes of architecture, all rolled into one to make art. This "art" is meant to last only a short time—its "idea" is the important thing. At the heart of such impermanent work is a renewed (not new) desire to get rid of the preciousness surrounding individual treasured objects, so as to place us all in step with the thinking of today's industrial mass society.

It's been suggested that especially the artists from Catholic countries (as Ferrer is) recognize the need for "desacrilization" of art which has been "worshipped" extensively in museums, as the achievement of genius, and collected by an elite few rich people. The "New Esthetics" would return art to the mass audience.

One step in this direction is to display art in the same place it's been produced, which has been done here—except that this elitist showcase indoors isn't a casual setting, and doesn't draw mass audiences. Another step is causing portions of the display to blend in with the permanent structure of the place in such a way that one can hardly distinguish which parts are temporary. This has possibilities, sometimes when the mass audience is actually being dealt with. Rafael Ferrer explains, "My work is concerned increasingly with creating spaces you can inhabit and spend time in." And that's the whole dramatic, stagey story in a nutshell.

Ferrer has created two major environments which visitors can enter, each containing structures that play on different levels of perception and reality. More primitive in feeling is the one having four huge freestanding units built of sticks ("class 10" telephone poles and lumber bolted together), a camping tent in one corner, some underbrush from his Mount Airy garden, and airport landing lights creating circular reflections on the room's 35-foot-high walls. The oily antiseptic odor of creosote from Bell Tel's poles is pervasive here, to the chagrin of some of the more staid occupants of the large building ICA shares with Penn's architecture department, among others. By the time you read this review, three tape recorders and an AM radio will be wafting contradictory sounds around.

The second environment is a partitioned space which becomes a labyrinth, consisting of various geometrically precise "sheds" reminiscent of pieced-together houses Rafael knew as a boy in Puerto Rico. Each shed has a few kinds of industrial materials in it—sheets of galvanized steel leaning against a wall or flat on the floor, neon handled mysteriously, a strong wooden rack with calves' skin draped across it, a transformer, TV sets turned on but without sound, a room with 80 slides of Puerto Rico being continuously projected.

As is often the case with Ferrer, the material equals the work. Both environments are quite controlled, the labyrinth more so. Subject to a number of diverse influences, Ferrer's eclectic work owes something to his contemporaries Morris, Sonnier, Smithson, Flavin. As I said, it's hard to tell where Ferrer's partitioned space leaves off and the permanent structure of the back-gallery room begins. About this, Ferrer says slyly, "The architects come and look, and it makes them uncomfortable unless they are very close to art. But then, what they do makes me uncomfortable."

Seems Ferrer is having his revenge against orthodox modern architecture—on his own behalf, and ours too. That's the most enjoyable feature of his work to me. What drives this point home is that the future plight of his work is exactly like so many architects' whose buildings get torn down so quickly in America—the only thing historians will have left of Ferrer's work after this show closes, and his steel goes back to the factory and his poles go back to Bell, will be photos. No pre-existing plans for Ferrer's work are shown, only the photo sequence made while his structures were in process of being built. These ironically will be kept and "treasured" as a unique art object might have been, to be reproduced some day doubtless, as photos of his other past projects are in ICA's exhibition catalogue. So the idea behind "Impossible" art isn't so different after all, and on top of that it leaves us, on the closing day of the show, once-removed from art with only our second-class relics.

One thing is certain—Rafael Ferrer, who is trying to do a little something for the spirit, has found himself a more sympathetic setting to make his audacious point than seemed the case at first glance. There's marvelous contradiction in all that wood-preservative smell emanating from Penn's modern citadel dedicated to learning about art, architecture, and our urban-rural environment. The younger Ferrer is witty and as much of a showman as brother José ever was. This new act will be hard to follow.

Chapter XXIII

COVERING THE HOMETOWN PERFORMER

At the risk of seeming to contradict earlier recommendations, I should like to suggest a modus operandi for reviewing the hometown performer—the town's "dramatic club," the high school or college play or even the village recitalist.

First of all, these comments apply when the performers are avowedly amateurs—that is, with no professional pretensions. This does not mean they have no ability; many amateurs can be of professional caliber. It does mean that they have no ambition to become professional actors or to go on the concert stage; they are giving this performance largely for the fun of it.

Of course, if the performance is of professional caliber, you have no problem! It is when the shortcomings equal or outweigh the virtues of the performance that the reviewer is ill at ease; he is uncomfortable not only from what he is watching and hearing, but also because he has to put his thoughts into writing.

Well, not all his thoughts—after all, there are libel laws! And you have to live with these people, too. How do you get around this difficult task?

My answer is simple: Accentuate the positive. Concentrate on the good points about the performance and write about them. This may seem at odds with the effort to "tell the whole truth and nothing but the truth," but you may translate it as being tactful. If the performers are friends or neighbors of yours—and in a small town this is quite likely—it would be difficult to rip an amateur performance apart and keep peace in the family. There is too much emotional involvement between performers and audience. The performers may be polite and say nothing, but they will hope you are not assigned to cover their next show. You may share this hope, but you may be the only staff member who covers the arts.

Covering the Hometown Performer

If the performance is so terrible that there is nothing good to say about it, you are entitled to sympathy both for having to watch it and having to write about it. If it is so bad that everyone, perhaps including the performers, realizes it, then you should feel free to pan it. Perhaps there are more talented performers available who were not used. This would be their cue next time.

Your review of the amateur play may well contain suggestions, direct or implied, as to how the next production may be improved. Beyond that, "accentuating the positive" means saying what good things you can, in conscience, say. Bad minor points may be ignored. Bad major points may be mentioned in reportorial fashion (without editorial comment) or may be dismissed kiddingly.

This chapter is being written in the light of the sage who prayed to help change things that could be changed, but who wished to be content with things that he could do nothing about. "Constructive" and tactful criticism may indeed inspire changes for the better when such changes are possible. It is when you would be asking for the impossible that "accentuating the positive" is recommended. If the town dramatic club insists on giving an "annual spring play," and their production isn't going to prevent a Broadway touring company from visiting the town, you may as well endure it. If the performers are the best available, hope that some will be genuinely worth praising. There are some areas in which adverse criticism may be warranted—such as poor taste in any phase of the production, including choice of the play itself. If there is possibility of improvement, by all means point it out: a better play that would still be within the capabilities of the troupe, or decor that does not measure up to the group's potential.

Covering a recital by the hometown musician may be more difficult to write about because you will be talking about only one performer, plus accompanist. "Accentuating the positive" is advised, let it be repeated, only when no professional ambitions are inherent—and this includes snaring music pupils. If Mme. Sharpe gives an annual recital in the hope of obtaining students for private lessons, your review should be as fully professional in your appraisal as her playing claims to be. Regardless of technique present or past, if her playing reflects little artistic merit, you would be doing a disservice to the art of music and to potential music students by praising this recitalist's playing and by implication recommending her as a teacher. Don't pull her chestnuts out of the fire. You cannot ignore it if the voice teacher sings flat or the violin teacher plays out of the tune.

If a young hometown musician gives a recital, you may be on the spot. It is important not to raise false hopes when there is little or no potential. Is the young musician giving this recital just for the fun of it or has he aspirations for the concert stage or opera? If the latter, he will be off to the conservatory in the big city—if he has talent. Do not mislead him. If his recital is an avowed or implied test of professional ability, give as honest a review as you can. You may very well say in so many words, in your review, whether—or not—young Boris Flatov has the potential for a concert career or should be dissuaded from such ambitions. Technique today is the norm; if Boris has little except technique, don't encourage him to a futile effort at a concert career. Naturally, if Boris is a genuine find, you will say so with pleasure.

Accentuating the positive is in order should the hometown church choir give a concert. With overaged sopranos and overripe bassos, this may be an ordeal. Your good comments may be necessarily restricted to the music itself rather than the performance—and, fortunately, there is no excuse these days for even the most amateur of choirs to perform bad music. Nor is there much excuse for lack of balance (unless the poor choir director has six sopranos and six altos, say, to every tenor and bass—and some directors have sopranos or altos sing tenor) or ragged attacks and releases. It is the quality of the voices themselves that may pain the critic's ear. "Accentuating the positive" is suggested here, as before, only if there is no immediate hope of drastic improvement; that is, if it is a small church, and the choir director is not young enough to be replaced easily or not old enough to retire. If the choral direction is bad, and there is the feasibility (as well as the artistic need) for a change, by all means let your review say so.

With a concert by the local college or high school choir you may reasonably expect and demand higher quality than that attained by the church choir. The voices are younger and more homogeneous. The singers are likely to be more alert and enthusiastic. Singer for singer, the school choir director is likely to get better results than with the church choir even if it is the same director.

The wealth of fine music in every category, for every age and ability, has raised the level of amateur programming. Few "glee clubs" sing only college, folk, and Broadway songs. Indeed, through foundation help there are composers-in-residence at colleges and in school districts, some of whom have been making significant contributions to the repertory for elementary, high school, and college choruses, bands, and orchestras.

Amateur ensemble concerts are usually punctuated, too, by the performance of one or more numbers by soloists or a small group, vocal or instrumental. Such groups, particularly the scholastic ones, nearly always have trick names, such as do barber shop quartets.

The town orchestra or band concert may also present problems to the reviewer. You should critically appraise the program choices not only as to musical worth but also as to whether they are within the capabilities of the players. A piece chosen for its brilliant conclusion may fall flat if the orchestra cannot play it. A key player or the whole ensemble may have trouble with only one or two passages. It's like the children's game of follow the leader—everybody could do all the stunts required except that 5-year-old Johnny couldn't quite make that four-foot jump over the puddle.

Your accentuating the positive may be strained here. Again, say nothing that is not true. Nor can faulty ensemble and out-of-tune playing be ignored. But do not expect depth of interpretation.

None of the foregoing should be interpreted as recommending that a performance should be praised if it is bad. Your overall verdict on the play, concert, or art exhibit should be as accurate as possible. In accentuating the positive, it is not intended that such comments imply that the performance (or the art exhibit) as a whole was good when it was not. The admonition is that the pen not write with vitriol; judiciousness may put your art of phrasing to the test.

Chapter XXIV

FINALE: OPPORTUNITIES AND PITFALLS

The opportunities for young reviewers were never greater. The "cultural explosion" all over the United States is providing more concerts than ever before; there are more community theaters, and more art exhibits, and there are more people wanting to read reviews about them. Moreover, there are community newspapers, some weekly, some daily, that would be grateful for qualified critics. TV and radio stations are also adding "critics-at-large" to their staffs.

In recent years a training program has evolved, with foundation help, for young music critics. They serve for a season as apprentices to established critics on metropolitan dailes. Such a program seeks to provide quality as well as qualified music critics, surely a worthy objective.

What are some of the pitfalls in being a practicing critic? The principal admonition here may scare off some stagestruck would-be critics: Avoid personal friendships with anyone about whom you may have to write. This means no more than a nodding, courteous acquaintance with actors, producers, playwrights, directors and other technicians, musicians, composers, conductors, opera singers.

To be emotionally involved with any arts professional that you must review is to tie your hands. Anything you write is suspect—you're "damned if you do and damned if you don't." You may give as dispassionate a review as is humanly possible, but you will be accused of either praising the performer because he is your friend, or "leaning over backward" and finding some fault, for the same reason.

Nor will you be able to write a dispassionate review of a friend's performance. You will want to praise him, and may be overly cognizant of less creditable details "in order to be fair." Your friend may deserve to be panned, but you hesitate to do so for fear of injuring your friendship.

It is one of the drawbacks of the critical profession that the people,

Finale: Opportunities and Pitfalls 143

except for other critics, with whom the reviewer would most like to associate, are automatically off ethical limits. But he may find congenial friends among doctors, lawyers, merchants, princes, candlestick makers, teachers, butchers, and bakers.

Of course there are exceptions. Critics have been known to maintain friendships with creative artists and performers despite reviews. They may even be married to a playwright or a concert artist. But on opening night someone else does the reviewing.

This maintenance of detachment is one of a critic's chief responsibilities. What are some of the others?

Oscar Thompson listed them in this order: "To the art of music, to himself, his readers, his employers, and those he writes about."

Notice what comes last in this listing. Music critics, especially, are considered fair game in some such reasoning as this: "The artist has worked so hard; you owe it to him to give him a review."

Neither the critic nor the artist owes each other anything. If the anticipated level of execution is high enough, if the program is worthy, if there will be a big enough audience to evidence public interest in the recital, if the critic's time and the newspaper's space are available—fine.

In other words, if for one or more reasons the concert is reviewed, the responsibility to the artist is only incidental, albeit an important incidental.

Thompson's rating of "the art" first is sound. If the critic, for whatever reason, is not entirely fair in his review—if he is too hard or too easy on a play, movie, TV show, concert, or art exhibit—he is not upholding the standard of the art of the drama, the cinema, television, music, or the fine arts.

Nor is he being fair to himself. If he rebels against his better judgment, if he temporizes in his review when his inner voice tells him otherwise, he is injuring his own status as a critic in addition to failing in his other responsibilities.

The conscientious critic has another responsibility to himself. He must always keep an open mind and never stop learning. He should be not only an insatiable reader about the arts but also should attend as many events in his and related fields as he can, whether "working" or not. To stop expanding his artistic horizon, to stop learning, is to stagnate. Then it is time for the paper to get another critic, one who has not lost his enthusiasm.

144   The Student Journalist and Reviewing the Performing Arts

The critic's obligations to his readers have been touched on throughout this book. Tell the whole story in clear language, giving descriptions and opinions as explicitly as possible. Bear in mind the publication for which you are writing. A review for a theatrical, art, musical, or broadcasting magazine may differ in content and language, though probably not in opinion expressed, from that in a newspaper.

Fulfillment of the above obligations automatically fulfills your obligation to your employer, assuming you follow your newspaper's writing style and get your reviews in on time.

Finally, the artist. He will be one of your most interested readers. And if your review has fulfilled its other responsibilities, its cogency will make him—enthusiastic or grudging—an admirer of yours.

Appendix A

A BASIC GLOSSARY OF ADJECTIVES AND ADVERBS

This is emphatically not a substitute for the dictionary. (It can't be.) It is merely an informal listing of words with various gradations of meaning, to serve not in themselves but to inspire you to consult a good dictionary, such as the Merriam-Webster *Collegiate,* or other word-building books such as Roget's *Thesaurus,* the Merriam-Webster *Dictionary of Synonyms,* or Crabbe's *Book of Synonyms and Antonyms.* By using the word with just the right shade of meaning you will speak more accurately and make your reviews more meaningful. Write your own additions to this list.

Note: Reading good literature is a vocabulary-builder, too.

Accurate: precise, exact.
Amusing: entertaining, rib-tickling, funny, uproarious.
Artistic: imaginative, musicianly, musical, dramatic, poetic, balanced, steady.
Awkard: clumsy, heavy-handed.
Balanced: steady.
Banal: trite, stereotyped, overworked.
Barely: hardly, almost, just about.
Believable: credible, convincing, cogent, valid, effective, able.
Breathtaking: speedy, rapid, lightninglike, scintillating, headlong, hasty.
Bright: brilliant, sunlit, dazzling, radiant, lustrous, scintillant.
Candid: frank, bare.
Clear: transparent, crystalline, luminous.
Colorful: flavorful.
Compassionate: sympathetic, empathetic.
Comprehensive: all-inclusive, encompassing.
Culpable: blameworthy.
Cumulative: kinetic, steadily growing in power.

Delineated: set forth, communicated, outlined.
Difficult: demanding, hazardous, tricky.
Dramatic: passionate, moving.
Dry: flavorless, arid, stuffy, brittle, strained.
Dull: listless, boring, uninspired, humdrum, monotonous, flat, under-keyed, understated.
Ebullient: spirited, buoyant, zestful, refreshing.
Excellent: fine, good, laudable, praiseworthy, commendable, distinguished, notable, perfect, eminent, creditable, lustrous.
Exciting: fiery, pyrotechnical, sparkling, scintillating.
Fanciful: imaginative, original, poetic.
Feathery: light, lightsome, ethereal, whispering.
Fresh: original, having a new treatment (or twist or angle), using a variation.
Golden: silvery, liquid, shining, brilliant.
Graphic: pictorial, vivid.
Grating: jarring, strident, harsh, coarse, raucous, rough.
Heavy-handed: unimaginative, steady, workmanlike.
Idiomatic: indigenous, inherent, native.
Incisive: penetrating, meaningful.
Introspective: thoughtful.
Intuitive: by nature, inherent, native.
Lively: spirited, viable, potent.
Long: lengthy, broad, wide, thick, unending, infinite, unceasing.
Martial: military, warlike.
Narrow: thin.
Opaque: turgid, cloudy, shadowed, shadowy.
Opulent: magnificent, eye-filling, splendid, extravagant, colorful, splashing, breathtaking, prodigal, rich, ample.
Peerless: unsurpassed, without equal.
Penetrating: perspicacious, well-thought-out, organized, structured.
Reticent: understated, whispered, subdued, muted.
Sharp: biting, pungent, acidic, astringent; angular, steep.
Shoddy: artificial, rickety, jerry-built, ersatz.
Small: tiny, miniscule.
Smooth: steady, unruffled, well-paced, silken.
Soft: gentle, whispered, floating, low, liquid, faint.
Sonorous: rich, resonant, full-throated, full-voiced, echoing, ringing.
Soothing: quieting.
Steady: well-paced, forward-moving, kinetic.
Strong: powerful, sturdy, rock-ribbed, well-founded, potent.
Triumphant: conquering.
Unique (none like it; stands alone): novel, unusual, rare.

Unnerving: disquieting, eerie, spooky.
Varied: differentiated.
Vigorous: powerful, sturdy, dynamic, energetic, potent, capable.
Violent: melodramatic.

Appendix B

STAGE AND FILM TERMS

Ad lib. An impromptu line inserted in a play's performance, usually for comedy effect or because of a minor emergency situation.

Angel or *Backer.* One who puts up some of the money to produce a stage play or musical. Usually the angel is a silent partner.

Billing. The form in which an actor's name appears in advertising a play or movie. The placing of the name and the exact size of type are specified in relation to the show's title and the names of other actors.

Book (noun). The spoken passages of a musical show; the plot (libretto). (verb). To schedule a movie or stage attraction into a showplace.

Burlesque. As used here, an old-fashioned kind of stage show featuring slapstick comedy and strip-teasers. Many burlesque comedians won later stardom in musical comedy, movies, and television.

Choreographer. The one who creates the dances for a show or ballet.

Credits. The listing of those who aid in putting on a play, movie, or other show—producers, director, designers, writers, etc.

Cue. The point in word or action when the next person speaks.

Decor (pronounced dayKOR). The visual aspects of a show, including both settings and costumes.

Director. The man who puts the actors through their paces. A movie director has a much wider influence than a stage director, since he may often be involved with the writing and editing of the script.

Extravaganza. A show, usually musical, with opulent decor.

Farce. A light comedy that is all but unbelievable.

Featured players. Those with billing below the rank of star.

Legitimate theater. An outworn term generally meaning stage plays or musicals of Broadway caliber. No one ever said what illegitimate theater was.

Libretto. The text of an opera, the "book" of a musical show.

Lighting. The scheme of illumination for a show, often involving technical creativity.

Lyrics. The words of the songs for a show, written by the lyricist.

Melodrama. Originally a romantic and sensational drama with musical interludes; now, a particularly strong and often violent drama.

Stage and Film Terms 149

Principal. One who has a leading role in a play, movie, or opera.

Producer. One in general charge of putting on a play or movie, hiring the director, creative artists, and performers. In the theater, he raises the money for the production.

Scenery or *sets* or *settings.* The visual background for a show, movie, ballet, or opera.

Star. The top performer, or one of a very few top performers, in a show. Technically, a star's name is billed above the title of the show.

Supporting role. One below the rank of featured player.

Tragicomedy. A drama blending comedy and tragic elements.

Tragedy. A drama of unhappy, even calamitous events.

Vaudeville. A variety show with comedy and musical numbers.

Waiting in the wings. Standing offstage, ready to go on.

Appendix C

A BASIC MUSICAL GLOSSARY

For the sake of completeness, some words have been included that anybody knows from general use, and a few such have been omitted. The definitions are aimed to help you in writing a review.

Absolute music. Music written for its own sake, with no story or picture attempted (see *Program music*).
A capella. Unaccompanied vocal music.
Accompanist. The pianist for a recital by another instrumentalist or a singer.
Acoustics. The science of sound. The tonal characteristics of a building. Good acoustics are advantageous to both performers and audience except for rock concerts.
Adagio. Slowly (see *Tempo*). Adagio can be the name of a movement of a symphony, concerto, or sonata.
Allegretto. Slower than Allegro.
Allegro. Quick, lively. It may also describe the movement of a major work. It may often be modified, as Allegro con brio (with spirit) or Allegro ma non troppo (quickly, but not too much so).
Alto. The low female voice. Short for contralto.
Andante. Slow, quiet, peaceful tempo.
Anthem. A sacred vocal composition, with or without accompaniment.
Aria. A solo number in an opera.
Arpeggio. Tones of a chord played in succession (broken chords).
Atonal. Without key or tonal center, using the tones of the chromatic scale impartially. Often characteristic of contemporary compositions.
Attack. Entry, which should be precise, of voices or instruments at the beginning of a composition.
Baritone. The medium male voice range, between bass and tenor.
Baroque. Music generally of the seventeenth century.
Bass. The lowest male voice; the bass violin, also called contrabass or bull fiddle or string bass; the lowest part of a musical composition.
Basso. A bass singer.

A Basic Musical Glossary

Basso buffo. A comic bass singer in opera. Don Basilio and Dr. Bartolo in *The Barber of Seville* are outstanding examples of such roles.

Bassoon. The double-reed bass member of the woodwind family.

Baton. The light stick with which the conductor beats time. It is as different from the drum majorette's baton as the conductor is from the drum majorette.

Beat. A division of a measure; the motion of the conductor's baton or hand in keeping time.

Bel canto. Literally (Ital.), beautiful song. Today it implies fine legato singing in the Italian style of a century or two ago, as opposed to the more declamatory style.

Bell. The flaring end of a wind instrument such as the horn and tuba.

Bow. The long implement of wood and horsehair used to play instruments of the violin family.

Bow-arm. The arm that holds the bow.

Bowing. The art of playing with the bow.

Brass. The family of brass instruments, including the French horn, trombone, trumpet, and tuba in the symphony.

Bridge. A thin piece of wood that supports the strings of the violin family.

Cadenza (Ital.). A long, brilliant passage played near the end of a concerto movement by the soloist. It may be written by the composer of the concerto or by someone else.

Canon. Imitation of the first voice's passage by succeeding voices. Canonic passages are frequent in choral and instrumental music.

Cantabile (Ital.). In singing style.

Carillon. A set of chimes played from a keyboard or with hands and feet from a console.

Castanets. Small hardwood clappers held in the hands, used to accompany some Spanish dances. If the Carmen is not adept with castanets, a man in the orchestra plays them for her.

Celesta. A small keyboard instrument with hammers that strike tuned metal plates. The sound is akin to a celestial chime.

Cello or *'Cello.* Abbreviation for violoncello.

Chord. Two or more notes sounded at the same time.

Chorus. A company of singers or would-be singers.

Chromatic. Presence of half-tones.

Clarinet. A single-reed woodwind.

Classical. The classical period is roughly the latter half of the eighteenth century. Classical music is all so-called serious music, as opposed to popular music.

Clef. A sign at the head of the staff to indicate the pitch of notes. The most common are the G or treble clef and the F or bass clef. Others are used for various instruments.

Coda (Ital., tail). A special closing to climax a composition.

Coloratura. Usually, coloratura soprano, one who can sing high ornamental passages.

Concertmaster. The principal first violinist in an orchestra. (In a band it is the first clarinetist.)

Concerto. A long composition, generally in three movements, for soloist and orchestra. Sometimes two or three soloists are used.

Console. The keyboards and stops of an organ.

Contrabass. The bass violin.

Contralto. Same as alto.

Contrapuntal. Use of counterpoint, combining related melodies with each retaining its linear character.

Crescendo. Gradual increase in tonal volume.

Cymbals. Brass plates that are clashed together.

Damper pedal. The "loud" pedal that raises the dampers from the piano strings, allowing the tone to be sustained.

Descant. A high obbligato in vocal music.

Decrescendo. Softening of the tonal volume.

Diapason. The organ stop that sounds the fundamental organ tone.

Diction. Enunciation of words sung in a musical composition.

Diminuendo. Same as decrescendo.

Dissonance. Unresolved chords. Most modern music employs some dissonance.

Divertimento. A piece or suite, generally of light character.

Double bass. The bass violin.

Double stops. Two notes sounded at the same time on a stringed instrument.

Dramatic soprano. A soprano who sings the heavier roles in opera, in the usual vocal range, as opposed to lyric or coloratura soprano.

Duet. A piece for two players or singers.

Duo. A pair of equal performers (not soloist and accompanist).

Dynamics. Degree of volume and quality of tone. A performer's control of dynamics is a measure of his musicianship.

E string. The highest of the four strings on the violin, and therefore the one most often used—and the one most liable to break during a concert.

Electronic organ. An organ that imitates the sound of a pipe organ by electronically amplified tones.

English horn. The tenor oboe, sounding a fifth below the regular oboe. The name is from the French, *cor anglais,* but is neither English nor a horn.

Ensemble. The entire body of performers. Qualitatively, the effect of this group in unity of purpose.

Entr'acte. An orchestral number between acts of an opera.

A Basic Musical Glossary

Etude (Fr., study). In concert, a short and often difficult piece for solo instrument.
F clef. The bass clef.
Falsetto. Artificial high tones of a voice, especially tenor.
Fantasia. A composition in free form.
Fingering. Use of the fingers in playing an instrument.
Flute. The soprano of the woodwind family. Nowadays flutes are usually of metal, perhaps silver or platinum, rather than wood.
Forte. Loud.
Fortissimo. Very loud.
French horn. The mellow-sounding brass instrument of the orchestra.
Frets. Strips of wood, metal, or ivory on the fingerboard of some string instruments, such as guitars and mandolins, to regulate the pitch.
Fugal (adj.). In the style of a fugue.
Fugue. A vocal or instrumental composition in which two or more musical lines are developed contrapuntally.
G clef. The treble clef.
G string. The lowest string on the violin. The name for the burlesque queen's essential garment was taken from this, rather than vice versa.
Glissando. A rapid connected passage played by sliding the fingers on a string instrument or the hand or fingers on the piano's white keys or the harp strings.
Glockenspiel. A set of small bells or steel bars played with rubber hammers, part of the orchestra's percussion family.
Guitar. The Spanish guitar of six strings, plucked, is the classical instrument. The Hawaiian or steel guitar is the popular variety.
Halftone. The smallest interval used in ordinary musical notation.
Harmonics. Soft, high tones produced by touching strings at certain nodal points.
Harp. An instrument of about 46 strings played by plucking the strings, whose pitch may be changed up or down half a tone by means of pedals.
Harpsichord. A keyboard instrument, displaced by the piano, with strings that are plucked instead of struck by hammers. Sometimes it has two manuals that may be coupled.
Heldentenor. A heroic tenor, who specializes in Wagnerian roles.
Horn. See *French horn.*
Impressionism. A school of musical composition, exemplified by Debussy, creating moods through rich harmonies and timbres.
Instrumentation. The instruments called for in a musical composition.
Intermezzo (inter-met-so). An entr'acte. Sometimes a short independent piece for piano or orchestra.
Interpretation. A soloist or conductor's conception of the music as shown in performance.

Interval. The difference in pitch between two sounds. Most music has regular intervals, but modern composers may make a singer or instrumentalist jump up or down more than an octave.
Intonation. Production of vocal or instrumental tone.
Jig. A lively dance, usually spelled Gigue (Fr.) or Giga (Ital.).
Kettledrums. See *Tympani.*
Key. The series of tones forming a major or minor scale.
Langsam. German for slow.
Largo. Very slow, stately, broad.
Legato (leh-GAH-to). Smooth and connected, with no break between tones. Legato playing or singing is important in phrasing.
Lento. Slow, between largo and andante.
Lied. German for song. Lieder in a concert means German art songs.
Lyric soprano. Between dramatic and coloratura soprano; she usually favors the roles for the latter.
Manuals. Organ keyboards.
Melody. An agreeable succession of single tones, rhythmically arranged; at any one time the leading part in a composition.
Mezza-voce. Half-voice (half its usual volume).
Mezzo-soprano. The range between alto and soprano. Most altos call themselves mezzo-sopranos nowadays.
Middle C. The note between the bass and treble clefs.
Modulation. The change from one key to another, preferably smoothly.
Motet. A sacred choral composition, usually unaccompanied, in contrapuntal style.
Motif. A musical phrase used to identify an operatic character (especially in Wagner) or as a theme for development in a composition.
Movement. A major division of a symphony, sonata, or concerto.
Mute. A small clamp placed on the bridge of string instruments to reduce the sound; also a cone placed in the bell of wind instruments for the same reason. When the tuba is muted it looks as if it's wearing a high hat.
Nachtstück. German for nightpiece, or nocturne.
Nocturne. A quiet, romantic piece.
Nonet. A piece for nine instruments.
Obbligato. Literally, essential to the performance of a composition, but actually an adjunctive part that may be more decorative than essential.
Oboe (Fr., hautbois—high wood; Eng., hautboy). A double-reed woodwind instrument. Its A often tunes the orchestra if a mechanical tuner is not used. Its sound often evokes a pastoral scene.
Octave. An interval of eight tones (from one lettered tone to another of the same name).
Octet. A vocal or instrumental group of eight performers, or a composition for eight.

A Basic Musical Glossary 155

Opera. A musical drama. (Also the plural of opus.)
Opus. Work. An opus number (Op.) ordinarily indicates its place in the chronology of a composer's output.
Oratorio. A major sacred choral composition, often with vocal solos.
Orchestra. A company of instrumentalists.
Organ. The "King of Instruments," consisting of thousands of pipes divided into ranks or stops, of varying tone colors, and played from a console with two or more manuals plus pedal keyboard. "Organ" usually refers to pipe organ but now may also mean electronic organ.
Overture. Usually the prelude to an opera, but there are many independent concert overtures, generally descriptive.
Part. The music assigned to a single voice or instrument, or group thereof.
Passacaglia (pahss-a-CAHL-ya). An old dance in three-four time usually on a ground-bass. Bach, Brahms, and others have used the passacaglia as a basis for variations.
Passage. A musical phrase or a brilliant run or arpeggio.
Passion. An oratorio on the last days of Jesus.
Pavan or *Pavane.* A stately dance in four-four time.
Pedals. The mechanism controlling the sound on piano or harp; a keyboard for the feet, on the organ.
Percussion. Orchestral instruments that are struck, such as tympani, drums, bells, cymbals, triangle, tambourine.
Phrasing. The punctuation of musical sentences for artistic effect.
Pianissimo. Very soft.
Piano. Soft. Also the usual term for pianoforte, the basic musical instrument.
Piano quartet. An ensemble of piano and three strings, usually violin, viola, and cello; also, a composition for this combination. A piano quintet is a work for piano and string quartet.
Piccolo. A small flute, an octave above the normal flute's pitch.
Pipe organ. See *Organ.*
Pitch. The relative position of a sound toward another sound or tone.
Pizzicato (pit-see-KAH-to; Ital., pinched). A direction for fiddlers to pluck the strings instead of playing with the bow.
Polyphonic. More than one voice in a composition.
Portamento. Gliding from one tone to another, usually vocal.
Prelude. An introduction to a major musical composition or to an act of an opera. Sometimes an independent piano work.
Presto. Fast.
Prima donna. The leading soprano.
Program music. Music that attempts to tell a story or depict a scene, as opposed to absolute music.
Quartet. Four performers, or a composition therefor.

Quintet. Ditto for five.

Rapport (ra-POR). Closeness of musical thought between performers.

Recitative. Free declamatory singing, often introducing an operatic aria.

Reeds. The reed instruments in an orchestra, the reed stops on an organ.

Registration. The management of stops by the organist.

Release. The ending (or cutoff) of a composition by an ensemble.

Requiem (Latin for rest). The first word of the requiem mass, hence often the title for such a work.

Rhapsody. A formless instrumental composition following the composer's fancy.

Rhythm. The regular pulsation of music, usually at equal intervals.

Romance or *Romanza.* A lyric instrumental piece, sometimes the slow movement of a sonata.

Romantic. Descriptive of music of expressive feeling, generally of the nineteenth century, between the classic and modern periods.

Rondo. A composition in which the first theme returns after each new theme. The final movement of a concerto is often a rondo.

Rubato (roo-BAH-to; It., robbed or stolen). Dwelling on one note and hurrying another, an effect often employed in romantic music. It should not be overused.

Run. A rapid passage, usually on the scale.

Sarabande. A stately dance in three-quarter time.

Saxophone. A brass instrument with clarinet mouthpiece, invented by Adolphe Sax of Belgium about 1840. It is used occasionally in a symphony orchestra.

Scale. The series of tones in any key.

Scherzo (SCARE-tzo). A jest; a sportive instrumental piece, often the lightest movement of a symphony.

Score. The music for all the parts of a composition, used by the conductor.

Septet. A composition for seven; an ensemble of seven musicians.

Serial. Arranged in a row; specifically, twelve-tone music that uses all the chromatic tones in the scale, though not necessarily in order.

Sextet. A composition for six; six performers.

Sinfonia. Nowadays it usually refers to an eighteenth-century orchestral suite, predecessor of the symphony.

Sonata. The highest development of musical form. Composition for one or two instruments, usually in three movements. Symphonies, quartets, and trios are usually written in the sonata form.

Soprano. The high female voice.

Staccato. Detached and distinct; notes played or sung separated from each other.

Stop. A set of organ pipes. Pressure of the finger on a fiddle string. *Double stops:* playing two notes at once (on two strings).

A Basic Musical Glossary 157

String quartet. The combination of two violins, viola, and cello; a composition for this ensemble.
String quintet. Usually, two violins, two violas, and cello.
Suite. A set of pieces of similar character with some contrast.
Symphony. A major orchestral composition, usually in four movements, each with its own themes and development.
Syncopation. Shifting the accent from the strong beat to the weaker one.
Technique (Technic, Eng.). The purely mechanical part of managing the instrument or voice.
Tempo. Time; the rate of movement. Major tempo indications: largo, adagio, andante, moderato, allegro, presto.
Tenor. The high male voice.
Tessitura. The general tonal range of a composition, which may be said to lie high or lie low for a voice. The finale of Beethoven's *Ninth Symphony* has a high tessitura for the vocalists.
Theme. A musical subject on which a fugue, set of variations, or part of a sonata is based.
Timbre. The quality of tone.
Time. The measurement of music by speed.
Toccata (It., touched). A brilliant keyboard composition in free style.
Tone. Sound or quality of sound.
Tone poem. A musical story, usually for symphony orchestra; Franz Liszt and Richard Strauss were its greatest composers.
Touch. The manner in which a player strikes the keys of a piano or organ.
Transcription. Arrangement of an instrumental or vocal composition for other than its original scoring. Leopold Stokowski's transcriptions of Bach organ works are among the most famous.
Transpose. To change to another key. Opera singers sometimes have arias transposed down a half-tone or a whole tone.
Treble. The high part in music.
Tremolo. The wavering of instrumental sound.
Trill. Rapid alternation of a note with the note a half or whole tone above.
Trombone. Brass instrument with a sliding tube that varies the pitch.
Trumpet. The brilliant brass instrument of the orchestra.
Tuba. The bass brass instrument.
Twelve-tone scale. All twelve chromatic tones of the scale. They are used, not necessarily in order, in modern compositions.
Tympani. The kettledrums, copper cups whose pitch may be raised or lowered by adjusting the parchment head. They are played in pairs or more.
Unison. Two or more instruments or voices sounding the same tone. If the singers or instrumentalists vary in pitch or time (in the same part) the ensemble will sound ragged or off-pitch.

Valves. The keys that change the pitch on wind instruments. Brass instruments have three valves.

Variations. Melodic and rhythmic modifications of a theme.

Vibrato. The resonant, wavering quality of string tone produced by the player's fingers on the strings. Too much vibrato is unwelcome in singing.

Viola. The alto of the fiddle family, a bit larger than the violin and tuned a fifth below.

Violin. The soprano of the stringed instrument family, and capable of the greatest expression.

Violoncello. The cello is tuned an octave below the viola. It ranks second to the violin as a solo instrument in the string family.

Virtuoso. A technically skilled instrumental or vocal soloist.

Vivace (vee-VAHCH-e). Lively, animated, rapid.

Vocalise (n.). A wordless concert piece usually for vocal solo.

Vocalize (v.). To practice vocal exercises, warming up before an opera or recital.

Voice. The sound produced by the human organ of speech. One part in a polyphonic vocal or instrumental composition.

Vorspiel. German for prelude, overture, introduction.

Vox humana. An organ stop imitating the human voice.

Whole tone. The normal step between notes.

Woodwinds. The flute and reed family in the orchestra—clarinet, bassoon, and oboe. A woodwind quintet also includes the French horn.

Xylophone. A set of tuned wooden bars played with small mallets, in the orchestra's percussion group.

Yodel. The Tyrolean warble.

Zither. A string instrument consisting of a shallow box with two sets of strings; the larger set is for accompaniment; the smaller set, fretted, is plucked to play the melody.

Appendix D

A BASIC BALLET GLOSSARY

Students who know French will have little trouble with ballet terms, since French is the language of ballet. The following terms should see you through. For more, consult a book on ballet.

Arabesque (from an Arabian intertwined ornamentation). A position in which the body is extended with one arm forward, the opposite leg backward.
Ballerina. Female dancer.
Ballet. A dance, in story or abstract, by a group.
Ballon. Feet stepping like a bouncing ball.
Batterie. The dancer's beating the feet together.
Bolero. A Spanish dance in three-quarter time.
Cabriole. High leap or caper.
Choreography. The composition of the dance. The one who devises the ballet is the choreographer. His name is paired first with that of the music's composer, e.g., Balanchine-Tchaikovsky *Serenade.*
Corps de ballet. The "chorus" or supporting group of the ballet company.
Coryphée. A leading dancer in the ballet corps.
Czardas. A Hungarian dance opening with a slow part (lassu) followed by the faster main part (friska). Liszt's Hungarian Rhapsodies are constructed thus.
Danseur noble. Principal male classic dancer.
Divertissement. A display piece either by itself or as part of a longer ballet.
Elevation. Height from the ground in dancing.
Entrechat. A leap in the air when the dancer crosses his feet before and behind each other alternately.
Fouetté. A turn on one leg, usually in series, with the other leg whipping through the air.
Galop. A lively French dance in two-four time.

Jota. A lively Spanish dance and song.
Lift. A male dancer's holding a ballerina in the air, in classical ballet.
Mazurka. A Polish dance in triple time.
Pas de deux. Dance for two. Grand pas de deux is a formal number by two leading dancers. (*Pas* literally means step).
Pas de trois. Dance for three.
Pas de quatre. Dance for four.
Pas de dix. Dance for ten.
Pirouette. Whirling or full turn on the toes, usually on one foot.
Position. A dance posture. There are five basic postures (*Les Cinq Positions*) of a ballet dancer.
Premiere danseuse. Principal female dancer of a ballet company.
Sur les pointes. On the toes.
Tableau. A grouping of dancers to form a stage picture.
Tutu. The short gauze skirts of the classic ballet costume, as in *Les Sylphides* and *Swan Lake.*
Variation. A classical ballet solo.

Appendix E

TELEVISION AND RADIO TERMS

AM. Amplitude modulation, 550 to 1600 on the AM radio dial.
Animations. Cartoon representations on television.
Audio. The sound part of a television broadcast.
CATV. An increasing field in television, providing specialized (coaxial cable feed) service to receivers in a certain area, or to areas that may have no other satisfactory TV reception.
Closed circuit. Television not on the air but within one or a few buildings, or only on network monitors.
Coaxial cable. The cable transmitting either network or CATV pictures and sound.
Commercials. As a noun, the sponsors' or public-service announcements at certain points in programs. They are generally of 60, 30, 20, or 10 seconds' duration.
Decibel. The unit for measuring loudness of sounds; the human ear's range is about 130 decibels.
Demographics. A broad term referring to sex, age, family, and economic characteristics of broadcast audiences.
Disc jockey. A radio personality who plays popular records on the air and gives news and entertainment interludes.
FCC. Federal Communications Commission, responsible for licensing TV and radio stations and overseeing broadcasting.
FM. Frequency modulation, 88 to 108 (megacycles) on the FM dial.
Live. A broadcast aired as it happens (not taped).
Location. Place of filming a show other than in the studio.
Net or *Network.* Connected stations presenting the same broadcast. A chain is several stations (not more than seven) under one ownership.
Pan. The usual theatrical term is to adversely criticize a show, but here it means to swing the camera to see a segment of a scene as a person might by turning his head.
Pilot. A sample show that may be telecast in the hope that favorable response will warrant its becoming a series.
Preempt. To replace a scheduled show, either by a network or an individual station, by another show of more immediate interest.

162   The Student Journalist and Reviewing the Performing Arts

Prime time. The evening broadcast hours when most people are watching television. It is usually from 7:30 to 11 P.M.

Program. An individual broadcast or a regular series, daily or weekly.

Rating. The percentage of homes in a broadcast area listening to a particular station or watching a certain program.

Remote. A broadcast originating away from the studio.

Script. The written text of a broadcast, play, or movie.

Segue (SAYG-way or seg). To make a smooth transition.

Series. A program telecast weekly or daily.

Share of audience. The percentage of tuned-in audience listening to a station or watching a program at any given time.

Special. A single program, generally of extra interest, that preempts a series episode.

Split screen. Showing of two or more separate scenes on the screen, in fractional display. The technique is often used in sports telecasting.

Sponsor. The advertiser who pays for all or part of the television or radio program.

Station break. The pause in a program, generally at the hour or half-hour, when the broadcasting station identifies itself and perhaps inserts local commercials.

Talk show. A program consisting primarily of interviews and/or discussions, on television. On radio the talk show may be between the host and listeners who telephone comments.

Tape. To record a TV or radio show on tape for future use. Most shows are taped, even if for use within an hour or two. The tape may then be edited for corrections and insertions and accurate timing.

Telemovie or *Teleplay.* A movie or play written primarily for television. If successful, it may be shown in theaters later.

UHF. Ultra high frequency, Channels 13 to 83 on the TV dial. Most noncommercial stations are UHF stations.

VHF. Very high frequency, Channels 2 to 12 on the TV dial. Most commercial stations are on these frequencies.

Video. The visual portion of a TV broadcast.

Appendix F

PERFORMING ARTS PERIODICALS PUBLISHED IN THE UNITED STATES

(Source: Ulrich's *International Periodicals Dictionary*, as of 1972)

ENTERTAINMENT

Action World. Guide to New York City and Long Island entertainment. Ten issues a year, $2. Book, film, and play reviews. Address: 327 Fifth Ave., New York, N.Y. 10017.

Billboard. Film, play, radio, television, and record reviews. Weekly, $30 a year. Billboard Publishing Co., 165 W. 46th St., New York, N.Y. 10036.

Carte Blanche. Book and record reviews. Biweekly. Los Angeles, Calif.

Cue. Film, play, and television reviews. Weekly, $9.50. Cue Publishing Co., 20 W. 23rd St., New York, N.Y. 10036.

Circus. Book, film, and record reviews. Monthly, $6. Address: 210 E. 52nd St., New York, N.Y. 10022.

Coast FM and Fine Arts. Book, film, play, and record reviews. Monthly, $6. Address: 291 S. Cienega Blvd., Beverly Hills, Calif. 90211.

Daily Variety. Movie, play, and television reviews. Five issues weekly, $30. Daily Variety, 6404 Sunset Blvd., Hollywood, Calif. 90028.

Hollywood Reporter. Book, film, and play reviews. Daily, $20. Tichi Wilkerson Miles, 6715 Sunset Blvd., Hollywood, Calif. 90028.

Star Time. Popular magazine. Bimonthly, $4. AAA Publishing Co., 201 Park Ave. S., New York, N.Y. 10003.

TV Guide. National and area television schedules, articles. Weekly, $7. Triangle Publishing Co., Box 400, Radnor, Pa. 19087.

TV Picture Life. Book, film, and record reviews. Monthly. Address: 315 Park Ave. S., New York, N.Y. 10010.

TV Radio Mirror. Popular monthly magazine. Address: 205 E. 42nd St., New York, N.Y. 10017.

TV Radio Movie Guide. Monthly, $4. Basic Women's Group, 6404 Hollywood Blvd., Hollywood, Calif. 90028.

TV Radio Show. Book and film reviews. Monthly, $4. Star Guidance, 315 Park Ave. S., New York, N.Y. 10010.

Television Quarterly. National Academy of Television Arts and Science, 1270 Avenue of the Americas, New York, N.Y. 10019.

TV Star Parade. Popular monthly magazine, $4.20. Ideal Publishing Co., 295 Madison Ave., New York, N.Y. 10017.
Variety. "The bible of show business." Film, music, play, radio, television, variety, and record reviews. Weekly, $20. Variety, 154 W. 46th St., New York, N.Y. 10036.

THEATER MAGAZINES

Bravo!. For the playgoer and concertgoer. Four to six issues yearly, $2.25. Bravo!, 3 E. 54th St., New York, N.Y. 10022.
Chrysalis. Pocket review of the arts, $2. Lily and Baird Hastings, 112 Vernon St., Hartford, Conn. 06106.
Drama Review Quarterly. New plays, criticism, theory, reviews, interviews, $6. New York University, 32 Washington Place, New York, N.Y. 10003.
Performing Arts. Book, film, and play reviews. Monthly, $10. K & K Publishing Co., 147 S. Robertson Blvd., Beverly Hills, Calif. 90211.
Show Business. Book and play reviews. Weekly, $15. Leo Shull, 156 W. 44th St., New York, N.Y. 10036.

MOTION PICTURE MAGAZINES

A B E L. Book, film, and play reviews. Monthly. Abel News Agencies, 300 W. 17th St., New York, N.Y. 10011.
Audience. Film and play reviews. Monthly, $3. Wilson Associates, 366 Carroll St., Brooklyn, N.Y. 11215.
Box Office. "The pulse of the motion picture industry." Weekly, $5. Associated Publishers, 825 Van Brunt Blvd., Kansas City, Mo. 64124.
Cinema (U.S.). Book and film reviews. Three years, $3.75. Spectator International, 9667 Wilshire Blvd., Beverly Hills, Calif. 90212.
CTVD: Cinema-TV Digest. Quarterly review of the foreign cinema-TV-press, $3. Hampton Books, Rt. 1, Box 76, Newberry, S.C. 29108.
Film TV Daily. Advance film reviews. Five issues a week, $20. Wid's Film and Film Folk, 330 W. 58th St., New York, N.Y. 10019.
Film Comment. Advance book and film reviews. Quarterly, $6. Film Comment Publishing Co., 100 Walnut Place, Brookline, Mass. 02146.
Film Quarterly. Book and film reviews, $5. University of California Press, Berkeley, Calif. 94720.
Film Society Review. Monthly (September to May), $5. American Federation of Film Societies, 144 Bleecker St., New York, N.Y. 10012.
Filmfacts. Reviews of U.S. and foreign films. Semimonthly, $25. American Film Institute, Box 213, Village Station, New York, N.Y. 10014.
Films in Review. Book and film reviews. Monthly, $7. National Board of Review of Motion Pictures, 210 E. 68th St., New York, N.Y. 10021.

Performing Arts Periodicals Published in the United States 165

Motion Picture Magazine. Film reviews. Monthly, $3. MacFadden-Bartell Corp., 205 E. 42nd St., New York, N.Y. 10017.

Movie Life. Fim, book, and record reviews. Monthly, $4.20. Ideal Publishing Corp., 295 Madison Ave., New York, N.Y. 10010.

Movie Mirror. Film and record reviews. Monthly, $3. Sterling Group, 315 Park Ave. S., New York, N.Y. 10010.

New Cinema Review. Reviews of independent, student, avant-garde, and underground films. September to June, $4. Box 34, New York, N.Y. 10012.

Photoplay. Film reviews. Monthly, $5. MacFadden-Bartell Corp., 205 E. 42nd St., New York, N.Y. 10017.

Show. Book, film, and play reviews. Monthly, $8. Show Publishers, 866 United Nations Plaza, New York, N.Y. 10017.

TV and Movie Screen. Book, film, and record reviews. Monthly, $4. Sterling Group, 315 Park Ave. S., New York, N.Y. 10010.

DANCE MAGAZINE

Dance Magazine. Book, film, and play reviews. Monthly, $10. Dance Magazine, 264 W. 47th St., New York, N.Y. 10036

RADIO AND TELEVISION MAGAZINES

Better Radio and Television. Quarterly. National Association for Better Radio and TV, 373 N. Western Ave., Los Angeles, Calif. 90004.

Communications Arts International. Published by International Association of Independent Producers, Leeward Publishers, Box 2801, Washington, D.C. 20013.

FM Music Program Guide. Book, music, play, and record reviews, and area FM programs. Monthly, $8. Address: 1290 Avenue of the Americas, New York, N.Y., 10019.

MUSIC MAGAZINES

American Record Guide. Monthly, $6. Box 319, Radio City Station, New York, N.Y. 10019.

American Musical Digest. Book, record, and music reviews. Monthly, $10. M.I.T. Press, Cambridge, Mass. 02142.

Changes. Book, film, and play reviews. Fortnightly, $11. Address: 120 E. 10th St., New York, N.Y. 10003.

Down Beat. Jazz magazine, with book and record reviews. Fortnightly, $8. Maher Publishers, 222 W. Adams St., Chicago, Ill. 60606.

High Fidelity/Musical America. Book, record, dance, and music reviews. Monthly, $14. Billboard Publishers, 165 W. 46th St., New York, N.Y. 10036.

166 *The Student Journalist and Reviewing the Performing Arts*

Gesture. Book, film, and music reviews. Bimonthly, $3. Box 1079, Northland Center, Southfield, Mich. 48075.

Jazz and Pop. Record reviews. Monthly, $6. Jazz Press, 1841 Broadway, New York, N.Y. 10023.

Listen. Tape, record, and film reviews. Bimonthly, $3. Rittenhouse Corp., 1808 Rittenhouse Square, Philadelphia, Pa. 19103.

Metropolitan Opera Program. Free. Saturday Review, 380 Madison Ave., New York, N.Y. 10017.

Music/AGO/RCCO Magazine. Reviews of books, organ, and choral music, records. Monthly, $7.50. American Guild of Organists, 630 Fifth Ave., New York, N.Y. 10020.

Opera News. Opera and record reviews. Weekly during season. Metropolitan Opera Guild, 1865 Broadway, New York, N.Y. 10023.

Philharmonic Hall Program at Lincoln Center. Free, monthly. Saturday Review, 380 Madison Ave., New York, N.Y. 10017.

Appendix G

EXAMPLES OF PLAY REVIEWS

My Fair Lady is used as the primary illustration of model reviews, both because it was—and is—a first-rate show, and it was written about in several categories: pre-Broadway, Broadway, movie, and revival.

The show had its world premiere in Philadelphia. Probably no one dreamed that it would set a Broadway record for musicals that would stand for more than twelve years until outdistanced by *Hello, Dolly!*

This show was in great shape for its pre-Broadway tryout, and the Philadelphia *Evening Bulletin* critic could find no fault with it. His review flows smoothly from one aspect of the show to another. The exceptional decor caused him to mention that first, after noting the Shavian basis of the libretto.

The reviewer names both the players and the characters they play; the latter are known to those familiar with Shaw's *Pygmalion*. He also tells a little of what the character does or is like. The "newcomer, a 21-year-old English girl" (in 1956) became a star with this show.

Non-German-speaking readers might object to the late Mr. Sensenderfer's last sentence, but the reviewer obviously thought the term familiar to enough of his readers.

* * *

Example No. 1

(From the Philadelphia *Evening Bulletin*, Feb. 16, 1959)

By R. E. P. Sensenderfer

"My Fair Lady" is the best musical this town has seen in years. If that sounds like too high praise, hustle off to the Erlanger Theater and see for yourself. It's a hundred-to-one shot you will agree.

168 The Student Journalist and Reviewing the Performing Arts

They have taken George Bernard Shaw's comedy in phonetics, "Pygmalion," and hewing closely to its Shavian satire and wit, have embellished it with a melodious and, at the same time, admirably fitting score by Frederick Loewe; and lyrics by Alan Jay Lerner that actually enhance in rhyme Shaw's own barbed arrows.

But that's not the half of it. Herman Levin has given it a production plus. There are no fewer than a dozen full stage sets of lavish beauty, by Oliver Smith, that flow into each other seemingly at the wave of a wand under Feder's spectacular lighting.

The scene is London in 1912 and Cecil Beaton, no less, has blended color with the period costumes in breathtaking profusion. If "My Fair Lady" did nothing but delight the eye, it would warrant a visit.

Does this overwhelm the play, you ask? Not in the least. Actually the performance, for the most part, pierces through the production; makes you almost unconscious of its glittering background.

Let's start with Rex Harrison, making his debut in a musical. Mr. Harrison, of course, can play Henry Higgins, the phonetics expert, with the best of them. But he can also sing; not with a big, operatic voice, to be sure, but with a phrasing that is a perfect blending of style and histrionics.

Right up with him is a newcomer, a 21-year-old English girl, Julie Andrews, whose Cockney flower-girl, Eliza Doolittle, is a thing of beauty and a joy throughout the evening. Her transition from a coarse and soiled grisette, through a maid of fashion at the Ascot races, up to the rigid formality of an Embassy Ball is Acting with a capital A. Her singing, and she has a sweet voice, matches Mr. Harrison in its manner.

Let's not forget Sidney Holloway's ribald, bibulous Cockney father, who succumbs to middle-class morality; nor Robert Coote's thoroughly British Colonel Pickering, who eggs Higgins on to his experiment in phonetics; nor Cathleen Nesbitt's warm dignity as Higgins' mother; nor Philippa Bevans' maternal housekeeper in Higgins' menage. Or, for that matter, Michael King's neat baritone as Eliza's love-sick but hopeless admirer. And all of these under the knowing direction of Moss Hart.

Now to get around to Hanya Holm's dance arrangements. There are no set ballets to interrupt the story line. But from time to time the buskers and Cockneys, bystanders and bartenders, street girls and society ladies burst into steps, acrobatic or stately, as befits the occasion and the song.

And don't forget those songs. They are all melodious and many have a neat way of changing tempo in the middle that is captivating. And the tunes are the kind you go out of the theater humming as in the old days.

"The Rain in Spain," capping the hilarious phonetics lesson, had them

Examples of Play Reviews

cheering last night. "With a Little Bit of Luck" is a lilting rough-house; "Wouldn't It Be Lov-er-ly" and "Get Me to the Church on Time" touch off lively dances, and the Ascot Gavotte and Embassy Waltz formal gliding. And for romance there is "On the Street Where You Live." There are a good round dozen in all and all are catchy.

And they aren't just sung as solos or duets or trios. They are usually acted out, as it were, and punctuated with little musical flourishes in the Russell Bennett orchestration, under Franz Allers' carefully modulated direction, as the singers switch.

So you can put down "My Fair Lady" as a rare treat; for its music, its story, its wit and, above all, for its exquisite taste. As a German would say, it is "sehr gemütlich."

Example No. 2

My Fair Lady opens on Broadway, and Brooks Atkinson praises the creative contributors before even mentioning the players. He also talks about several supporting actors before getting around to the two stars. Broadway reviewers do not always acknowledge the existence of the theater elsewhere. *The New York Times* critic's lead is unusual in that it gives credence to the out-of-town tryout reports.

*   *   *

Bulletins from the road have not been misleading. "My Fair Lady," which opened at the Mark Hellinger last evening, is a wonderful show.

Alan Jay Lerner has adapted it from Shaw's "Pygmalion," one of the most literate comedies in the language. Many other workmen have built the gleaming structure of a modern musical play on the Shaw fable. They are Frederick Loewe, the composer who collaborated with Mr. Lerner on "Brigadoon" and "Paint Your Wagon"; Oliver Smith, who has designed a glorious production; Cecil Beaton, who has decorated it with ravishingly beautiful costumes; Moss Hart, who has staged it with taste and skill.

Although their contributions have been bountiful, they will not object if this column makes one basic observation. Shaw's crackling mind is still the genius of "My Fair Lady." Mr. Lerner has retained the same ironic point of view in his crisp adaptation and his sardonic lyrics. As Professor Higgins and Eliza Doolittle, Rex Harrison and Julie Andrews play the leading parts with the light, dry touch of top-flight Shavian acting.

"My Fair Lady" is staged dramatically on a civilized plane. Probably for the first time in history a typical musical comedy audience finds itself absorbed in the art of pronunciation and passionately involved in the proper speaking of "pain," "rain" and "Spain."

•

And yet it would not be fair to imply that "My Fair Lady" is only a new look at an old comedy. For the carnival version adds a new dimension; it gives a lift to the gaiety and the romance. In his robust score, Mr. Loewe has made the Covent Garden scenes more raffish and hilarious. Not being ashamed of old forms, he has written a glee-club drinking-song, and a mock hymn for Alfred Doolittle's wedding.

Not being afraid of melody, he has written some entrancing love music, and a waltz, and he has added something to Professor Higgins' characterization in a pettish song entitled "A Hymn to Him." All this is, no doubt, implicit in "Pygmalion." But Mr. Loewe has given it heartier exuberance. Although the Old Boy has a sense of humor, he never had so much abandon. "Pygmalion" was not such a happy revel.

•

In the choreography and in the staging of the musical numbers, Hanya Holm has made a similar contribution. The "Ascot Gavotte" at the races is a laconic satire of British reserve in the midst of excitement, and very entertaining, too. "The Embassy Waltz" is both decorous and stunning. And to the rollicking tune of "Get Me to the Church on Time" there is a rowdy, festive dance that is vastly enjoyable.

Despite all the rag-tag and bobtail of a joyous musical show, Mr. Hart and his associates have never lost their respect for a penetrating comedy situation. Some things of human significance are at stake in "My Fair Lady," and some human values are involved. Thanks to the discerning casting, the values have been sensitively preserved. As Professor Higgins' sagacious mother, Cathleen Nesbitt carries off her scenes with grace and elegance.

•

As Alfred P. Doolittle, the plausible rogue, Stanley Holloway gives a breezy performance that is thoroughly enjoyable. And Robert Coote is immensely comic as the bumbling Colonel Pickering.

But it is the acting of Miss Andrews and Mr. Harrison in the central roles that makes "My Fair Lady" affecting as well as amusing. Miss Andrews does a magnificent job. The transformation from street-corner drab to lady is both touching and beautiful. Out of the muck of Covent Garden something glorious blossoms, and Miss Andrews acts her part triumphantly.

Although Mr. Harrison is no singer, you will probably imagine that he is singing when he throws himself into the anguished lyrics of "A Hymn to Him" in the last act. By that time he has made Professor Higgins' temperament so full of frenzy that something like music does come out of him. Mr. Harrison is perfect in the part—crisp, lean, complacent and condescending until at last a real flare of human emotion burns the egotism away and leaves us a bright young man in love with fair lady. Mr. Harrison acts his part triumphantly, too.

It's a wonderful show. To Shaw's agile intelligence it adds the warmth, loveliness and excitement of a memorable theatre frolic.

Example No. 3

My Fair Lady had become familiar in legend, if not otherwise, by the time it paid its first return visit to Philadelphia nearly five years after its world premiere.

The Philadelphia Inquirer reviewer assumes most readers know about the show, yet he tactfully takes little for granted. (See Chapter XII.)

* * *

(From *The Philadelphia Inquirer,* Dec. 6, 1968)
By Henry T. Murdock

First things first. "My Fair Lady" is back and she's as fair as ever. If you didn't meet her when she was here nearly five years ago, you are in for one of the musical comedy thrills of the current era. If you are seeing her for another time, you will marvel at her freshness and her spirit and her melodious charm.

In short, the production which opened Monday night comes as close to capturing an original impact as any return engagement could possibly achieve.

The cast is top grade in every particular. If the lavish beauty of the production has been touched at all, the results are not visible.

Alan Jay Lerner's distillation of Bernard Shaw's "Pygmalion" is a prize libretto adroitly retaining the substance and much of the expression of the original play while gracefully wedding it to the musical comedy form.

As for Frederick Loewe's music (and Lerner's lyrics), the songs bubble out as though they were inspired yesterday and sung for the first time today by an exuberant cast that didn't know or didn't care how many recordings had been sold. And sung, incidentally, to an audience in the same frame of mind.

As the old gag has it, the Monday night customers must have started

172 The Student Journalist and Reviewing the Performing Arts

applauding when they bought their tickets. They kept it up to the exit music.

The "fair lady" herself is played by Caroline Dixon, English songstress making her official debut in the role after a couple of "sneak previews" during the Baltimore engagement.

She has a ringing voice which can give the bravura accent to "Just You Wait, 'Enry 'Iggins" and "Show Me," the plaintive notes to "Wouldn't It Be Loverly?" and "I Could Have Danced All Night," and the spirit of triumph to "The Rain in Spain."

In point of performance, she is probably more Shaw and less Lerner than Julie Andrews, who created the role, and by the same token gives perhaps a little more force to the libretto. She delivers the famous Ascot scene tag-line with artistic vehemence.

It seems logical that in seeking successors to Rex Harrison, astute director Moss Hart should try to match appearance as well as quality and, in Michael Evans, Mr. Hart has succeeded on both counts.

However, Evans is far from a mimic. He has a better voice than his illustrious predecessor, exhibits the same blind and comic nonchalance and does fine things to "I'm an Ordinary Man" and "I've Grown Accustomed to Her Face."

And if you thought Stanley Holloway couldn't be replaced as Alfred Doolittle, you should see and hear Charles Victor stop the show completely with "With a Little Bit of Luck" and "Get Me to the Church on Time."

Reid Shelton gives "The Street Where You Live" more prominence than it ever had before; Hugh Dempster is an amusing Colonel Pickering and Hanya Holm's choristers have that original fervor.

Example No. 4

It was more than eight years after its Broadway premiere that *My Fair Lady* was finally released as a movie.

This review by "Land" from Variety, the weekly "bible" of show biz, tells not only of the merits of the show itself, but also gives some facts and figures—and predictions—of special interest to the trade.

* * *

The great longrun stage musical made by Lerner & Loewe (and Herman Levin) out of the wit of Bernard Shaw's old play, "Pygmalion," has now been transformed into a stunningly effective screen entertainment. "My Fair Lady" in Technicolor and Super Panavision 70 must

Examples of Play Reviews 173

clean up for Warners. It has riches of story, humor, acting and production values far beyond the average big picture. It is Hollywood at its best, Jack L. Warner's career capstone and a film that will go on without now-foreseeable limits of playoff in reserved seat policy and world rentals.

That Warner paid $5,500,000 for the rights alone is a staggering first fact. Add that after $20,000,000 the original stage production interest collects 47½% of the net. So a lot of people are going to again make it to the bank from this Midas musical.

Care and planning shine in every detail and thus cast a glow around the name of director George Cukor. Of course the original staging genius of Moss Hart cannot be overlooked as a blueprint for success. But like all great films "My Fair Lady" represents a team of talents. The delicate task of proper apportionment of credits will draw different answers but this reviewer would rate Rex Harrison's performance and Cecil Beaton's design of costumes, scenery and production as the two powerhouse contributions. Which, of course, in no way neglects appreciation of the master eye behind the camera, to wit, Harry Stradling.

Alan Jay Lerner's screenplay derived from his own stage libretto has not attempted to improve on a hit, although there is some rearrangement, compression and telescoping for cinematic effects. Some of the action is "opened up." The color of London before World War I benefits through the camera creation of both working and upper class customs.

Gene Allen's art direction probably constitutes a major credit, even within the master-plan of Beaton. Francis J. Scheld and Murray Spivack handled the sound, a mighty undertaking. A plus value for the widescreen version is that anybody may sit anywhere and hear every lyric and see every facial nuance. An important aid to the over-all impression is the editing of the footage by William Zeigler, which is exceptionally smooth, although there are a number of sharp jumps of locale.

This is a man-bullies-girl plot with story novelty. An unorthodox musical without a kiss, the audience travels to a total involvement with characters and situation on the rails of sharp dialog and business. The deft segues of dialog into lyrics are superb, especially in the case of Harrison. One can only guess the preparation and takes necessary to get the effect. Technical maps and paraphernalia incident to Higgins' scientific work in phonetics have been given much attention. It enhances the verbal obsessions of the Harrison role upon which all is based.

Main credit, following a prolonged garden of flowers, stars the title rather than Audrey Hepburn and Rex Harrison, who are billed below the show, and hence not strictly within the defined conditions of stardom. Some may wonder why Harrison is subordinate to the girl in the billing since he dominates "My Fair Lady" as he dominated "Cleopatra."

Only incurably disputatious persons will consider it a defect of "Lady" on screen that Julie Andrews has been replaced by the better known Miss H. She is thoroughly beguiling as Eliza though her singing is dubbed by Marni Nixon.

Stanley Holloway repeats from the Broadway stage version. Again and again his theatrical authority clicks. This great English trouper takes the basically "thin" and repetitious "With a Little Bit o' Luck" and makes it stand up as gaiety incarnate.

Everyone in the small cast is excellent. Mona Washbourne is especially fine as the prim but compassionate housekeeper. Wilfred Hyde-White has the necessary proper gentleman quality as Pickering and makes a good foil for Harrison. Gladys Cooper brings aristocratic common sense to the mother of the phonetics wizard. The lovesick young man who sings outside the house, and is otherwise just a tenor from sub-plot, has been assigned to Jeremy Brett. He photographs handsomely and sings with nice melody. The Hungarian charlatan speech expert who nearly upsets the masquerade at the high style ball is plausibly handled by Theodore Bikel.

The staging of the fashionable paddock scene at Ascot closely approximates the tableau used on the stage, though enlarged. Elsewhere in the picture there are a number of freeze-action bits but in general the story is told with strict realism, albeit dressed to the burst of Beaton's imagination. Women must dote on the gowns. All will be struck by the comfort and service for the well-to-do of the England that was. The house in which Higgins lives and where most of the action takes place is sheer recapture of a bygone era.

Hermes Pan cleverly handled the choreographic movement essential to some of the songs, which travel all over the sets. The ballroom detail is of high style detailing.

A certain amount of new music by Frederick Loewe and added lyrics by Lerner are part of the adjustment to the cinematic medium. But it is the original stage score which stands out. Actually the numbers never went out of fashion so all that may reasonably be said is that a fresh peak of popularity may follow in the wake of the picture. Andre Previn handled the orchestra using arrangements of Alexander Courage, Robert Frankly and Al Woodbury.

Running some 10 minutes short of three hours "My Fair Lady" is a long film but only rheumatics will object to sitting that long. There is hardly a dull moment and, more to the point, there are many laughs, many humanly touching scenes, and song numbers that come smashing through. Audience applause must break out during the unspooling.

This is an occasion for general congratulations. Hollywood has seldom looked lovelier.

Examples of Play Reviews 175

Example No. 5

Now the movie version of *My Fair Lady* reaches Broadway. *The New York Times* reviewer acknowledges the similarities of stage and screen versions, especially in casting, yet he "accentuates the positive." (See Chapter XIV.)

* * *

(From *The New York Times,* Oct. 22, 1964)
By Bosley Crowther

As Henry Higgins whooped, "By George, they've got it!" They've made a superlative film from the musical stage show, "My Fair Lady"—a film that enchantingly conveys the rich endowments of the famous stage production in a fresh and flowing cinematic form. The happiest single thing about it is that Audrey Hepburn superbly justifies the decision of the producer, Jack L. Warner, to get her to play the title role that Julie Andrews so charmingly and popularly originated on the stage.

All things considered, it is the brilliance of Miss Hepburn as the Cockney waif who is transformed by Prof. Higgins into an elegant female facade that gives an extra touch of subtle magic and individuality to the film, which had a bejeweled and bangled premiere at the Criterion last night.

Other elements and values that are captured so exquisitely in this film are but artful elaborations and intensifications of the stage material as achieved by the special virtuosities and unique flexibilities of the screen.

There are the basic libretto and music of Alan Jay Lerner and Frederick Loewe, which were inspired by the wit and wisdom in the dramatic comedy, "Pygmalion," of George Bernard Shaw. With Mr. Lerner serving as the screen playwright, the structure and, indeed, the very words of the musical play as it was performed on Broadway for six and a half years are preserved. And every piece of music of the original score is used.

There is punctilious duplication of the motifs and patterns of the decor and the Edwardian costumes and scenery, which Cecil Beaton designed for the stage. The only difference is that they're expanded. For instance, the Covent Garden set becomes a stunningly populated market, full of characters and movement in the film; and the embassy ball, to which the heroine is transported Cinderellalike, becomes a dazzling array of regal splendor, as far as the eye can reach, when laid out for ritualistic emphasis on the Super-Panavision color screen. Since Mr. Beaton's decor was fresh and flawless, it is super-fresh and flawless in the film.

In the role of Professor Higgins, Rex Harrison still displays the egregious egotism and ferocity that he so vividly displayed on the stage, and Stanley Holloway still comes through like thunder as Eliza's antisocial dustman dad.

Yes, it's all here, the essence of the stage show—the pungent humor and satiric wit of the conception of a linguistic expert making a lady of a guttersnipe by teaching her manners and how to speak, the pomp and mellow grace of a romantic and gone-forever age, the delightful intoxication of music that sings in one's ears.

The added something is what Miss Hepburn brings—and what George Cukor as the director has been able to distill from the script.

For want of the scales of a jeweler, let's just say that what Miss Hepburn brings is a fine sensitivity of feeling and a phenomenal histrionic skill. Her Covent Garden flower girl is not just a doxy of the streets. She's a terrifying example of the elemental self-assertion of the female sex. When they try to plunge her into a bathtub, as they do in an added scene, which is a wonderfully comical creation of montage and pantomime, she fights with the fury of a tigress. She is not one to submit to the still obscure customs and refinements of a society that is alien to her.

But when she reaches the point where she can parrot the correct words to describe the rain in Spain, she acknowledges the thrill of achieving this bleak refinement with an electrical gleam in her eyes. And when she celebrates the male approval she receives for accomplishing this goal, she gives a delightful demonstration of ecstasy and energy by racing about the Higgins mansion to the music of "I Could Have Danced All Night."

It is true that Marni Nixon provides the lyric voice that seems to emerge from Miss Hepburn, but it is an excellent voice, expertly synchronized. And everything Miss Hepburn mimes to it is in sensitive tune with the melodies and words.

Miss Hepburn is most expressive in the beautiful scenes where she achieves the manners and speech of a lady, yet fails to achieve that one thing she needs for a sense of belonging—that is, the recognition of the man she loves.

She is dazzlingly beautiful and comic in the crisply satiric Ascot scene played almost precisely as it was on the stage. She is stiffly serene and distant at the embassy ball and almost unbearably poignant in the later scenes when she hungers for love. Mr. Cukor has maneuvered Miss Hepburn and Mr. Harrison so deftly in these scenes that she has one perpetually alternating between chuckling laughter and dabbing the moisture from one's eyes.

This is his singular triumph. He has packed such emotion into this film—such an essence of feeling and compassion for a girl in an all-too-human bind—that he has made this rendition of "My Fair Lady" the most eloquent and moving that has yet been done.

There are other delightful triumphs in it. Mr. Harrison's Higgins is great—much sharper, more spirited and eventually more winning than I recall it on the stage. Mr. Holloway's dustman is titanic, and when he roars through his sardonic paean to middle-class morality in "Get Me to the Church on Time," he and his bevy of boozers reach a high point of the film.

Wilfred Hyde-White as Colonel Pickering, who is Higgins's urbane associate; Mona Washburn as the Higgins housekeeper, Gladys Cooper as Higgins's svelte mama and, indeed, everyone in the large cast is in true and impeccable form.

Though it runs for three hours—or close to it—this "My Fair Lady" seems to fly past like a breeze. Like Eliza's disposition to dancing, it could go on, for all I'd care, all night.

Example No. 6

Now it's twelve years after the premiere. *My Fair Lady* is known to anyone who goes to plays or movies.

This was the first nonprofessional production of the show in Philadelphia, performed by college and post-college players under a director known for his high standards. The reviewer was prepared to make allowances, both in production and performance, but it was unnecessary.

* * *

(From *The Philadelphia Inquirer,* July 6, 1968)

By Samuel L. Singer

"My Fair Lady" is no show for amateurs or semi-pros—except Dan Rodden's Music Theater of La Salle College. Rodden's array of talent more than meets the challenge of the Lerner-Loewe hit as their first production of the summer in the college's Union Theater.

"My Fair Lady," the long-running "musical of the century" that gave rise to so many legends about how hard it was to obtain tickets, is a difficult work to stage on several counts.

178   *The Student Journalist and Reviewing the Performing Arts*

First of all, there's the matter of Eliza Doolittle's believable transformation from Cockney flower-girl to young society miss in speech and looks. Pretty Fran Spiegel, young French teacher at La Salle and an experienced amateur thespian, accomplishes both metamorphoses brilliantly. She can sing and dance, too.

While not neglecting the other principals, another production hurdle is the ensembles, such as the Ascot races, the Transylvania Embassy Ball, and the song hit, "Get Me to the Church on Time." Costume designer Gerard Leahy has wrought eye-filling gowns for the ball and has perfectly pictured the Ascot event with gray ensembles for the men and black and white dresses with absolutely fabulous hats for the women. The hearty song "Get Me to the Church on Time" is outstanding.

Eliza's role and the professionally performed ensembles are merely highlights in an all-around production that easily upholds Rodden's high standards. James J. Christy, a better singer than Rex Harrison, is brusque but not violent as Professor Higgins, who works the transformation in the libretto based on Shaw's "Pygmalion."

Mustachioed Joseph F. Leonardo is a rather mousy but effective Colonel Pickering. Patrick J. Cronin makes the most of the flavorful role of Alfred Doolittle, Eliza's imbibing father.

Other roles are well taken by Donald Shannon as Freddy, Eliza's suitor who sings "On the Street Where You Live"; Henrietta Whyte as Mrs. Pearce, the sympathetic housekeeper; Barbara Myer, as Colonel Higgins' mother, and James Harvey as Zoltan Karpathy, his nosy former student.

Leahy's flexible sets match his costumes in imagination. Anthony Mecoli conducts an excellent 12-piece orchestra. The singers and dancers perform energetically, with choreography by Robert Wilson and Mary Woods Kelly making good use of the crowded stage.

"My Fair Lady" is fair and a real lady in this newest Dan Rodden production.

Appendix H

BIOGRAPHICAL DATA

Identifying capsules of the more prominent composers, writers, artists, etc., mentioned in the pages of this book.

Anderson, Maxwell (1888-1959). American playwright, b. in Atlantic, Pa.
Arlen, Michael, *orig.* Dikran Kouyoumdjian (1895-1956). British novelist and playwright, b. in Bulgaria of Armenian parents.
Arp, Jean (1887-1966). French sculptor, painter, and poet, b. in Strasbourg.
Bach, Johann Sebastian (1685-1750). German composer, b. in Eisenach.
Bacon, Francis (1561-1626). English philosopher and author, b. in London.
Barrett, Elizabeth (1806-61). English poet, b. in Durham.
Barrie, James M[atthew] (1860-1937). Scottish novelist, b. in Kirriemuir.
Beethoven, Ludwig van (1770-1827). German composer, b. in Bonn.
Behrman, S[amuel] N[athaniel] (1893-   ). American playwright, b. in Worcester, Mass.
Berlin, Irving, *orig.* Israel Baline (1888-   ). American composer, b. in Russia.
Berlioz, [Louis] Hector (1803-69). French composer, b. in La Côte-Saint-André.
Bizet, Alexandre César Léopold, *called* Georges (1838-75). French composer, b. in Paris.
Brahms, Johannes (1833-97). German composer, b. in Hamburg.
Brancuși, Constantin (1876-1957). Rumanian sculptor, b. in Pestisani-Gorque.
Browning, Robert (1812-89). English poet, b. in Camberwell.
Buck, Pearl S[ydenstricker] (1892-1973). American novelist, b. in Hillsboro, W. Va.
Cézanne, Paul (1839-1906). French painter, b. in Aix-en-Provence.
Chaliapin, Feodor Ivanovitch (1873-1938). Russian basso, b. in Kazan.
Channing, Carol (1923-   ). American musical comedy star, b. in Seattle, Wash.
Chopin, Frédéric François (1810-49). Polish-French pianist-composer, b. near Warsaw.

180 The Student Journalist and Reviewing the Performing Arts

Congreve, William (1670–1729). English playwright, b. in Bardsey.
Connelly, Marc[us Cook] (1890–   ). American playwright, b. in McKeesport, Pa.
Coward, Noël (1899–1973). English actor, playwright, and composer, b. in Middlesex.
Debussy, [Achille] Claude (1862–1918). French composer, b. in Saint-Germain-en-Laye.
Degas, [Hilaire Germain] Edgar (1834–1917). French painter and sculptor, b. in Paris.
Diabelli, Antonio (1781–1858). Austrian composer, b. in Mattsee near Salzburg.
Donizetti, Gaetano (1797–1848). Italian operatic composer, b. in Bergamo.
Dorsey, Jimmy, orig. James Francis (1900–57). American bandleader and clarinetist, b. in Shenandoah, Pa.
Dorsey, Tommy, orig. Thomas Francis (1905–56). American bandleader and trombonist, b. in Mahanoy Plains, Pa.
Duchamp, Marcel (1887–1968). French painter, b. near Rouen.
Dumas, Alexandre (1824–95). French playwright, b. in Paris.
Faulkner, William (1897–1962). American novelist, b. in New Albany, Miss.
Fauré, Gabriel Urbain (1845–1924). French composer, b. in Pamiers.
Ferber, Edna (1887–1968). American novelist, b. in Kalamazoo, Mich.
Fitzgerald, F[rancis] Scott [Key] (1896–1940). American novelist, b. in St. Paul, Minn.
Flagstad, Kirsten (1895–1962). Norwegian dramatic soprano, b. in Hamar.
Friml, [Charles] Rudolf (1881–1972). Bohemian-born American composer, b. in Prague.
Gershwin, George (1898–1937). American composer, b. in Brooklyn, N.Y.
Gielgud, John (1904–   ). British actor, b. in London.
Gilbert, William Schwenk (1836–1911). English playwright, b. in London.
Gogh, Vincent van (1853–90). Dutch painter, b. in Groot-Zundert.
Gounod, Charles François (1818–93). French composer, b. in Paris.
Handel, George Frederick (1685–1759). German composer, b. in Halle; became naturalized British subject, 1726.
Harrison, George (1943–   ). Youngest member of the Beatles, b. Liverpool, England.
Harrison, Rex (1908–   ). British stage and screen star, b. Huyton, England.
Hart, Moss (1904–61). American playwright, b. in New York City.
Haydn, [Franz] Joseph (1732–1809). Austrian composer, b. in Rohrau.

Biographical Data 181

Hayes, Helen (1900–). American actress, b. in Washington, D.C.
Hepburn, Audrey (1929–). Hollywood actress, b. in Brussels, Belgium.
Herbert, Victor (1859–1924). Irish-American composer, b. in Dublin.
Hemingway, Ernest (1899–1961). American novelist, b. in Oak Park, Ill.
Howard, Sidney Coe (1891–1939). American playwright, b. in Oakland, Calif.
Ibsen, Henrik (1828–1906). Norwegian dramatist, b. in Skien.
Joyce, James (1882–1941). Irish novelist, b. in Dublin.
Kaufman, George S[imon] (1889–1961). American playwright, b. in Pittsburgh, Pa.
Kelly, George (1887–). American playwright, b. in Philadelphia, Pa.
Kreisler, Fritz (1875–1962). Austrian-American violinist-composer, b. in Vienna.
Lahr, Bert, *orig.* Irving Lahrheim (1895–1967). American comedian, b. in New York City.
Lennon, John (1940–). Member of the Beatles, b. in Liverpool, England.
Lewis, Ted. *orig.* Theodore Lewis Friedman (1891–1971). American bandleader and clarinetist, b. in Circleville, Ohio.
Liszt, Franz von (1811–86). Hungarian pianist-composer, b. in Raiding.
Mahler, Gustav (1860–1911). Austrian composer, b. in Kalischt.
Massenet, Jules Émile Frédéric (1842–1912). French composer, b. in Montaud.
Matisse, Henri (1869–1954). French painter, b. in Le Cateau.
McCartney, Paul (1942–). Member of the Beatles, b. in Liverpool, England.
Menotti, Gian-Carlo (1911–). Italian-American composer, b. in Cadegliano.
Meyerbeer, Giacomo *orig.* Jakob Liebmann Beer (1791–1864). German-French composer, b. in Berlin.
Miller, [Alton] Glenn (1904–44). American bandleader, b. in Clarinda, Iowa.
Mozart, Wolfgang Amadeus, *orig.* Johannes Chrysostomus Wolfgangus Theophilus (1756–91). Austrian composer, b. in Salzburg.
Muni, Paul, *orig.* Muni Weisenfreund (1895–1967). American stage and screen actor, b. in Lemberg, Austria-Hungary.
Mussorgsky, Modest Petrovich (1839–81). Russian composer, b. in Karevo.
O'Neill, Eugene Gladstone (1888–1953). American playwright, b. in New York City.
Paganini, Nicolò (1782–1840). Italian violinist-composer, b. in Genoa.
Picasso, Pablo [Ruiz y] (1881–1973). Spanish painter and sculptor, b. in Málaga.

Porter, Cole (1893–1964). American composer, b. in Peru, Ind.
Prokofiev, Sergei (1891–1953). Russian composer, b. in St. Petersburg.
Puccini, Giacomo (1858–1924). Italian operatic composer, b. in Lucca.
Ravel, Maurice Joseph (1875–1937). French composer, b. in Ciboure.
Rice, Elmer Leopold, *orig.* Reizenstein (1892–1967). American playwright, b. in New York City.
Robinson, Edward G. *orig.* Emanuel Goldenberg (1893–1973). American actor, b. in Bucharest, Rumania.
Romberg, Sigmund (1887–1951). Hungarian-American composer, b. in Szegedin.
Rubinstein, Artur (1889–   ). Polish pianist, b. in Lódź.
Saroyan, William (1908–   ). American playwright, b. in Fresno, Calif.
Scarlatti, Domenico (1685–1757). Italian composer, b. in Naples.
Schubert, Franz Peter (1797–1828). Austrian composer, b. in Vienna.
Seurat, Georges (1859–91). French painter, b. in Paris.
Shakespeare, William (1564–1616). English dramatist, b. in Stratford-on-Avon.
Shaw, George Bernard (1856–1950). British playwright, author, and critic, b. in Dublin.
Sherwood, Robert Emmet (1896–1955). American playwright, b. in New Rochelle, N.Y.
Starr, Ringo (1940–   ). Tympanist, member of the Beatles, b. in Liverpool, England.
Stokowski, Leopold Antoni Stanislaw (1882–   ). Orchestra conductor, b. in London, England.
Strindberg, August (1849–1912). Swedish playwright, b. in Stockholm.
Sullivan, Arthur Seymour (1842–1900). English composer, b. in London.
Synge, John Millington (1871–1909). Irish playwright, b. in Rathfarnham.
Szell, George (1897–1970). American orchestra conductor, b. in Budapest, Austria-Hungary.
Tauber, Richard (1892–1948). Austrian tenor, b. in Linz.
Tchaikovsky, Peter Ilich (1840–93). Russian composer, b. in the Ural region.
Toscanini, Arturo (1867–1957). Italian orchestra conductor, b. in Parma.
Verdi, Giuseppe (1813–1901). Italian operatic composer, b. in Parma.
Vivaldi, Antonio (1675?–1741). Italian violinist-composer, b. in Venice.
Wagner, [Wilhelm] Richard (1813–83). German composer, b. in Leipzig.
Weber, Karl Maria Friedrich Ernst von (1786–1826). German composer, b. in Eutin.
Williams, Tennessee, *orig.* Thomas Lanier (1911–   ). American playwright and author, b. in Columbus, Miss.
Yeats, William Butler (1865–1939). Irish dramatist, b. near Dublin.

LB
3621
.S54

Singer, Samuel L.

The student jour-
nalist and re-
viewing the per-
forming arts

DATE DUE

JUL 11 '89			